HENRY WOODMAN

THE HISTORY OF VALLEY FORGE

WITH A BIOGRAPHY OF THE AUTHOR AND THE AUTHOR'S FATHER WHO WAS A SOLDIER WITH WASHINGTON AT VALLEY FORGE DURING THE WINTERS OF 1777 AND 1778

❊ THIRD EDITION ❊

Henry Woodman

Authorized by the Woodman Family

HERITAGE BOOKS
2025

HERITAGE BOOKS
AN IMPRINT OF HERITAGE BOOKS, INC.

Books, CDs, and more—Worldwide

For our listing of thousands of titles see our website
at
www.HeritageBooks.com

A Facsimile Reprint
Published 2025 by
HERITAGE BOOKS, INC.
Publishing Division
5810 Ruatan Street
Berwyn Heights, MD 20740

Copyright © 1921 John U. Francis, Sr.

Originally Published by
John U. Francis, Sr.
Oaks, Pa.
1921

— Publisher's Notice —

Page 102 and 103 are missing.

In reprints such as this, it is often not possible to remove blemishes from the original. We feel the contents of this book warrant its reissue despite these blemishes and hope you will agree and read it with pleasure.

International Standard Book Number
Paperbound: 978-0-7884-3789-2

GENERAL WASHINGTON

PRESS OF
THE EXPRESS PRINTING CO.
LITITZ, PA.

PREFACE

A LARGE portrait of a plain, unassuming man was hanging on the wall of the old Camp School-house in Valley Forge park, when John U. Francis, Sr., publisher of this history, took charge. Father was born in Lower Providence township, just across the Schuylkill river from the Cradle of American Liberty. His great-grandfather, Captain Arnold Francis, had commanded the Providence militia and had rendered conspicuous service under Washington at Valley Forge. In the family, Valley Forge was sacred ground and to the name of Washington was rendered a homage hardly due to mortal man. In keeping with the suffering endured, a resentment toward British arrogance was developed which even to-day causes the eye to flash at the slightest semblance of the thing on our national horizon. A patriotism purer than father's we have never met. To tell the story of Valley Forge, than whom no man knows it better, and to provide for visitors to the park suitable souvenirs has been to him a labor of love. The publication of this history is a becoming climax of his labors.

But year after year the portrait continued to hang on the wall. When at times we visited the Park and inquired, Whose is that portrait? practically no light could be given. "It was sent down from Headquarters." Some one knew better than father. In the summer of 1919 a group of visitors entered the School-house. One of the ladies pointed to the portrait and said: "That is a portrait of my grandfather, Henry Woodman. He wrote the first history of Valley Forge." The lady was Mrs. Alice Woodman Smith of Wycombe, Bucks county, Pa. She promised a letter giving particulars, and in due time one was received. Miss Mary S., daughter of Henry Woodman, a lady now of some eighty summers, was the embodiment of the first commandment with promise. She had had a small portrait of her father enlarged and had sent it to the Headquarters at Valley Forge. As already stated, from there it was sent down to the old Camp School-house.

Henry Woodman, after many years of urging, wrote his history of Valley Forge. His home was now near Doylestown, Bucks county, Pa. It was in 1850 that he wrote, and for The Doylestown Intelligencer. It appeared in the shape of letters for thirty-two consecutive weeks, from April 30 to December 3. There is internal evidence that the history at that time awakened national interest. It seems to have been copied by other newspapers. Woodman was requested to print it in book form, but never did so. Through his granddaughter, Mrs. Smith, it was learned where the text of his history could be found. Invaluable service and utmost courtesy were received from the Historical Societies of Montgomery and Bucks counties; and acknowledgements for the same are herewith made. The book as now published is authorized by the Woodman family.

The advice of John W. Jordan, LL.D., historian of the Valley Forge Park Commission, seems to us to be good, viz., that we leave Woodman tell his own story, his whole story, and without any attempt at editing. Consequently no editing has been done. Woodman himself in one of the last letters, says that if the history were published in book form, he would make some grammatical corrections. Evident errors of this nature have been corrected, but it is believed that in no way has the individuality of the writer been marred.

As to the unique fitness of Henry Woodman to write the history of Valley Forge, we refer you to the sketch of him by his daughter, Miss Mary S. Woodman, p. 16 and then to the sketch of his father, Edward Woodman, p. 11 also by Miss Mary S. Woodman. But the book must be read to perceive his surpassing fitness. His mother is his heroine. She was nineteen years of age when the army encamped at Valley Forge, and she resided within the lines of the encampment. She was recognized in her day as a living history of it.

It has been urged against Woodman that he received his information in his earlier years, that he wrote at the age of fifty-five, and after he had been away from Valley Forge for a quarter of a century, that he wrote only from memory, without any official papers at hand. In reply we beg to say that he had been told the stories o'er and o'er in youth by his father, who had been a soldier in the camp here, who tramped with him over the old encampment grounds from his fifth year and upward, and the father's delight was to explain to his son. He had heard his mother ever and anon tell of "those times." Henry later took visitors over the grounds and acted as informant, reiterating the stories told him. He had heard the old ladies, lasses at Valley Forge in 1778, recount in conclave to each other encampment reminiscences. Bring up a child in the way in which he should go and when he is old he will not depart from it. Beside his mother lived up almost to the time that he wrote; and his mother's sister was still living. This sister was nine years old at the time of the encampment and was a favorite of Baron DeKalb. At the time of writing Woodman interviewed others who had lived at Valley Forge during the memorable time. Also he had helped old soldiers who had been there to get pensions and had assisted others in securing money from the government for damages incurred through the encampment. Furthermore, he frequently discussed Valley Forge matters with men of intelligence, of patriotism, and of affairs. He had been a school teacher, a scrivener, a surveyor at Valley Forge, and a Quaker preacher, all of which tended to make him capable, exact and conscientious, and consequently more reliable. He wrote when he was mature and before his faculties were impaired. Who can doubt that Providence prepared him for his task? Surely his history may be received with confidence.

The Quaker has been stigmatized as pro-Tory. Valley Forge was a Quaker settlement. William Penn had given his daughter Letitia a manor here of more than 1000 acres; and she in 1705 built what it now known as the old Camp School-house, at present the quarters of the publisher of this history. Here Henry Woodman attended school; and it is most fitting that his history should now go forth from its walls to educate the nation on Valley Forge. The Quakers were opposed to war; as a class they were second to none in devotion to the interests of the colonies. If some were pro-Tory, this cannot be said of Henry Woodman. His father, an Episcopalian by birth, practically a Quaker or Friend at death, was through the Revolution from start to finish, from Carolina to Massachusetts. No purer American blood ever flowed than that which coursed through the veins of Henry Woodman. His was red blood, but not too red. His love for Valley Forge is exactly the spirit toward it that should be fostered in American homes. Valley Forge is our national center. Woodman is an expression of American life, not a superimposition upon it. His history should be in every American home.

He gives the history of Valley Forge from the time his ancestor Evan ap Bevan in 1686 took up here 2000 acres of virgin land, down through the Revolution to the time he wrote the history. Some parts will be found of more interest than others. He not only introduces us to but causes us to form the acquaintance of the generals of Washington's army. Baron DeKalb was quartered at the home of Woodman's grandfather. If the Frenchman Lafayette was wounded for our independence, for our independence the Prussian DeKalb made the supreme sacrifice; also Baron Von Steuben, another Prussian, made Washington's army strong unto invincibility. But we must uphold Poland for Kosciusko's sake, and for the sake of Pulaski, who, DeKalb, laid down his life for us. We can hardly forgive Lafayette for not coming to Valley Forge when he visited America. Every true American rejoices that we could pay our debts to France and Poland; but read and answer to your own conscience whether we owe a debt to Prussia. The World War is over, and the words of Lincoln are suited to every American: "With malice toward none, with charity for all." We are sure that this is the spirit of Woodman's history of Valley Forge.

J. G. FRANCIS.

Lebanon, Pa., Feb. 12, 1920.

PREFACE TO THE THIRD EDITION

SOME errors of grammar and some of fact crept into the first edition. These have been corrected as far as we have been able to detect them. This edition is much more profusely illustrated, and misplacement of illustrations has been rectified. A few small additions have been made to the preface of the first edition, it being deemed better to place them there than in this preface. A Table of Contents and an Index have also been added, as well as a list of Illustrations. Some of the headings in the body of the book have been changed and some have been added, presenting, we believe, a better grasp of the book. What was an Introduction has been made an Appendix. The map of the Park was added already to the second edition.

As to the identity of the quarters of the generals, we take Woodman as authority. He possessed every means of knowing, and he was above misrepresentation. There is no one whom we regard as at all comparable to him in this matter. Where any one clearly differs from him, we at once discard them. This will cause a revolution as to some acceptations; but our course will, we are sure, set wrong acceptations right as surely as did the Revolution. Practically every one who has done any service in determining these locations, whose work has come to our notice, we are confident ultimately drew chiefly from Woodman.

While Woodman knew and is accepted as knowing, his designations will be worthless unless we can identify them. It was seventy years after the Revolution when he wrote, and it is seventy years since he wrote. The farms had changed hands many times up to when he wrote, and they have changed hands many times since. They have been divided and subdivided. In many cases the original buildings have been torn down and have been succeeded once or twice by new ones. On new farms formed from parts of the old, buildings have been erected which in some cases are much older than the new buildings which succeeded the original ones on the old farms. It will thus be seen that our problem becomes intricate. Had we left ourselves open in the least to discouragement, again and again we would have given up the task. We persevered till the clouds broke and rolled away; and we believe that over our head is now a clear sky.

We believe in the traditions of a worthy people; and none are more worthy than the Quaker farmers of "the Great Valley" about Valley Forge, under whose roofs Washington and his generals found shelter during the awful winter, the fateful winter, of 1777-78. To doubt the traditions of these people falls not short of treason. To doubt them is to nullify the value of Valley Forge Park. Who will sufficiently estimate the influence of their simple faith in carrying Washington and his noble band safely through the crucial ordeal? The general who stood next to Washington himself was a regular attendant of the Quaker meetings. He drank from fountains that strengthened. The Quaker's Sword of the Spirit wrought more than the sword of steel. We thank God that the ground of Valley Forge Park, the mecca of our national birth, has received not one drop of brother man's blood that cries out to God for vengeance.

But back to the tangible. We want to give credit to those descendants of "ye olden time" Quaker farmers of "the Great Valley," who helped us to identify the farms of which Woodman tells.

First, we called on "Bill" Stephens, whose ancestor's farms quartered so large a part of the army and also Generals Varnum and Huntingdon. There is no question as to the identity of these farms. "Bill" was born under the roof which sheltered Varnum. Treat him tenderly, considerately for the sake of his fathers.

To Charles Havard of Lebanon, Pa., prothonotary of Lebanon county, born also under a roof that sheltered one of Washington's generals, we are indebted for directing us to those who helped us. Clarence Roberts, who is a mixture of all the old Quaker families, and whose farm is a part of the Knox quarter farm, helped us to identify the quarters of Knox, Woodford, Scott and Greene. The four farms on which were Potter, Poor, Mifflin, and Sullivan are the four farms in a sense generally accepted, but they have become obscured and confused among themselves. In unthreading the tangle, we are indebted to Nathan Walker and to the Richards brothers and sister. The History of the Walker Family by Mrs.

The History of Valley Forge

Streets afforded no little help in all these cases. Mrs. Peter Rapp of Oaks, Pa., whose husband's great-grandfather died at Valley Forge, and whose mother, a born Kennedy, was reared on the Mordecai Moore farm, bears testimony as to the identity of that place.

The other quarters are not in doubt, and the general acceptation accords with our author, likely came from him. Several of the generals were quartered in huts, among them Baron Von Steuben. There is a tradition that in the later stage of the encampment, the Baron was quartered in a little stone house now sandwiched in between the higher stone part and the high brick part of what was the residence of Gen. Fisher, near the Village of Valley Forge, the property now owned by Heinz of the 57 kinds of food preparation; but our author does not mention this and we pass it by. Woodman was of the impression that officers were quartered across the river; but as he was never able to clear up the matter, no one has ever made anything of it. We advance the theory that Armstrong was across the river. We hope that the trans-river problem will yet be cleared up.

We had entertained the hope of interviewing Rev. Quimby of Berwyn, a few miles south of Valley Forge, on the South Valley Hill, who has written an interesting romance on Valley Forge. After we had reached our conclusions, our hope was gratified. The beautiful, the magnificent view of the Great Valley from his South Valley Hill lured him into writing the story. He weaves in so many authentic incidents that his story may to some extent be accepted as a history of the encampnent. But he had read Woodman in full. Mr. Campbell, now deceased, of Berwyn, had succeeded in doing what we did later, though without our knowledge till our call on Rev. Quimby—Mr. Campbell had succeeded in copying with his own hand all of Woodman's History. Rev. Quimbly is not an original investigator. He accepted current traditions and wrote his story. But Mr. Campbell did more than copy Woodman. He spent a lot of time and money in locating and photographing the quarters of the generals. His conclusions do not all agree with ours, but his list deserved to overflowing the distinction accorded it by the Valley Forge Park Commission, viz., of being printed in their report of 1904. We were gratified to find that Mr. Campbell placed Scott where we had placed him.

We deem it in place here to say something in particlar about the quarters of Knox and Mifflin, for here we run up against generally accepted tradition. Woodman tells us that Maxwell was quartered on the farm now accepted as Knox's quarters and now owned by his worthy descendant, United States Senator Philander C. Knox. Woodman places Knox on the farm joining this one on the south, now owned by Thos. Royal. The error we account for in this way: It became customary in old diagrams to mark only the quarters of Knox to the southwest of the encampment, Maxwell being left out, it being known that Knox was to the southwest, the first farm in that direction was assigned as his quarters. Woodford was also to the southwest, but because others were omitted, he also has been placed on a wrong farm. All must receive their due, if any are to be kept in their proper place.

Mifflin is assigned to the "Little White Cottage," Miss Thomson's convalescent home for children, on the Thomson estate. This was the main house of the Benj. Jones farm just bought from Jacob Walker and still occupied by him. (See page 119). At his house Potter was quartered. See page 58. Benjamin Jones occupied the other house "with a few acres of land." Here Poor was quartered, doubtless after having been with Pulaski on the Beaver farm. This home of Benjamin Jones must have been the old part of the house now occupied by Nathan Walker, which Nathan thinks stood at the time of the Revolution. Woodman clearly places Mifflin on the Havard Walker farm now owned by Commissioner John R. K. Scott. Sullivan was on the farm north of this, also owned by Mr. Scott, the buildings being on the Richards Road. The original houses on both these farms are no longer standing. The old house between Sullivan's quarters and Mr. Scott's summer residence, the Children's Summer Home, was built in 1791.

Had time and means permitted, further investigations might with profit have been made. We have done what we could and believe the quarters of the generals have been correctly identified. Like all people American, we are open to amendment.

The sale of two editions in the Old Camp School-house the first year is very gratifying to the publisher and his friends, and demonstrates that this text-book on Valley Forge meets a need and that this aspiration to educate the nation on Valley Forge is well under way.

It has become our conviction that this history was written on the request of Washington himself, for on his last visit to Valley Forge in 1796, just before laying aside his mantle of public service and retiring to Mt. Vernon, Washington came to our author's father, plowing in the field, and asked for information concerning the place. See page 126. Our author was then less than a year old. The father reared his son for the task which he must have perceived Washington wished performed. Who can doubt that "the Father of his Country" regarded Valley Forge as the realization of the birth of the nation, the place where the prayer of suffering endurance touched the heart of God and caused Him to present to us our priceless gift of national independence, in that freedom wherewith his Son makes free. John 8:36.

Washington said to the father of our historian that "to see the people happy and satisfied, and the desolate fields recovering . . . . . . afforded him more real satisfaction than all the servile homage that could be paid to his person or station." These words should be preserved in stone or metal in the field in which they were uttered. Surely to have the government administered in the spirit of Philadelphia and Valley Forge would afford him more pleasure than to have the government located in a city or to have a President sail the ocean in a ship called by his name, however respectful these courtesies may be.

Heaven is a place as well as a condition, and the condition is assured with certainty only in the place; and the continuance of the government in its original purity is assured only in the place of its birth. The location of the site of our government in a province originally settled by a part of the Christian Church with headship across the ocean points us to one thing only—subjection to foreign domination. Continued possession of the liberty won by the prayer of suffering of Washington and his heroic band is assured with certainty only by the seat of the government in the place of its birth, in the City of Brotherly Love, down past which flows the waters of Valley Forge.

Because of these things we cannot in vain invoke God's blessing on this book as it goes forth more fully on its mission. God bless it in the name of our Lord Jesus Christ. Amen.

J. G. FRANCIS,

Lebanon, Pa., Jan. 20, 1921.

TABLE OF CONTENTS

Preface	7
Life of Henry Woodman	19
Author's Introduction	24
Valley Forge in 1850	27

Before the Encampment

Original Settlement and the Forge	28
A Depository of Military Stores	30
The Burning of the Valley Forge	33
Hunting Jehu—Two Women of the Revolution	33
Unceremonious Visit of the Hessians	39
Phin's Fort	41
General Observations	42
Dewee's Regalia	42
Howe and Burgoyne	44
Lydia Darrach and Another "Female"	45

The Encampment Proper

Arrival of the Army	49
Locating the Encampment	53
Quarters of the General Officers	57
Disposition of the Army	59
Incidents of the Camp	62
More About Wheedon	66
DeKalb Succeeds Wheedon	67
Other Distinguished Foreigners	70
Dubryson's Cave	70
Steuben's Kitchen	71
Sullivan's Bridge	72
Sufferings of Civilians	74
Soldiers as Beasts of Burden	74
Hospitals	75
About Some of the Officers	76
Alarms and Losses	79
The Hanging of a Spy	79
A Duel	80
Some Addenda	81
"Benevolent Females"	83
Later Celebrities	83
The Forts	85
Bake-House and Armory	86
Provision Store	87
Before and After	87
The British Informed	88
Departure and Desolation	91
A Few Reflections	93
A Community Prostrate	95

The German Physician and the Riding Horse............. 96
From War to Peace.................................. 97
SUBSEQUENT TO THE ENCAMPMENT
The Forge Relit....................................... 99
The Headquarters after the War....................... 100
The Disposition of the Potts' Estate.................... 101
Other Land West of the Creek......................... 104
An Indian Tale 105
Across the River..................................... 107
  The Pauling Estate................................ 107
  The Wetherill Estates.............................. 107
  The Mines near Shannonville (Audubon)............. 108
  Two Guests of James Vaux.......................... 109
  The Bakewell Home and Audubon.................... 109
  A Traveler's Estimate of this Section................. 110
East of the Valley Creek.............................. 111
  The Farm of John Brown........................... 111
  The Farm of Samuel Havard........................ 112
  The Farm of John Havard.......................... 112
  Richards and Jones Farms.......................... 113
  Farm of John Beaver............................... 115
  Farms of Joseph Walker............................ 116
  About Gen. Wayne................................. 116
  The Farm of Benj. Jones............................ 119
  Farms of Thomas Waters........................... 119
  The Widow of Col. Dewees Indemnified.............. 120
  Farm of Abijah Stevens............................. 121
In the County of Montgomery
  West of the River.................................. 123
  The Moore Properties.............................. 123
  Alexander Kennedy 123
  A Dignified Visitor in a Plain Suit of Black........... 126
  Letitia Penn's Manor............................... 128
  The Jenkins-Morris Farm........................... 128
  Port Kennedy 129
  The Provost Farm.................................. 133
  The David Stephens Farms.......................... 136
Minerals 138
General Review 143
New Timber Growth................................. 143
Pilgrimages and Gatherings........................... 145
Visit of Lafayette.................................... 146
Conclusion 149
Heroines of the Story................................. 149
A Son's Hero.. 150
Concluding Requests 151
Author's Valedictory 153
Biography of Edward Woodman....................... 157

ILLUSTRATIONS

	Facing Page
Henry Woodman, the Author, frontispiece	3
General Washington	4
Quarters of Wheedon and of DeKalb	38
Birthplace of the Author	38
Old Camp Schoolhouse, exterior	39
Old Camp Schoolhouse, interior	39
The March to Valley Forge	48
In Winter Quarters at Valley Forge	49
Washington's Headquarters	56
Interiors of Washington's Headquarters (5)	57
Generals of the Army	76
The Nation's Message	77
Quarters of the P. O. S. of A.	100
Quarters of Gen. Varnum and of the D. A. R.	100
Quarters of Gen. Huntingdon	101
Quarters of the Provost Guard	101
Von Steuben drilling the Soldiers	106
The Vaux-Bakewell-Wetherill Mansion	107
The Saylor-Francis Home	107
Quarters of Gen. Maxwell	110
Quarters of Gen. Lafayette	110
Quarters of Gen. Knox	111
Quarters of Gen. Lee	111
Quarters of Gen. Scott	114
Quarters of Gen. Woodford	114
Quarters of Lord Sterling	115
Quarters of Gen. Pulaski	115
Quarters of Gen. Wayne	118
Quarters of Gen. Greene	118
Quarters of Gen. Potter	119
Quarters of Gen. Poor	119
Quarters of Gen. Mifflin	122
Quarters of Gen. Sullivan	122
Quarters of Gen. Morgan and Com.-Gen.	123
Quarters of Gen. Muhlenberg	123

THE LIFE OF HENRY WOODMAN

BY

HIS DAUGHTER, MARY S. WOODMAN

EARLY LIFE

Henry Woodman, the third son and fifth child of Edward and Sarah (Stephens) Woodman, though born at the Valley Homestead on the 20th of December, 1795, cannot be said to have grown up in his parents' household. The greater part of his childhood and youth was spent with his grandmother and aunts at their home about half a mile farther up the creek (Valley Creek on which is Valley Forge), in the house built by Grandfather Stephens after the Revolutionary War.

Being industrious, willing, quick-minded, and always prompt, when things were given him to do, all the errands of both homes fell to his luck. Of things Father told me of his child life he could not have been a boy as others were, the sports and amusements of other children had no charm for him and he would not engage in many of them. The consequence was that others, having more of the bad boy in them, had often made a butt of him for their cruel fun. Possessing, as he did, a mind of keen sensibility, he suffered much from the jokes of his companions. Every opportunity for the improvement of his mind was eagerly sought after; and, by the time he was fourteen had made so much progress in all that was taught in the neighboring school, his relatives thought it right to send him to a boarding school. Money was hard to get—could they meet the costs? "Well," said his father to Aunt Becky Stephens, "by all means *we must* educate Henry, for he does not know enough ever to make anything but a scholar." The various kinds of work that called for farm or mechanical skill Henry could not learn, and that is why his father thought him fit only for a scholar.

SCHOOL-TEACHER, ACCOUNTANT AND SCRIBE

So it came to pass, when the summer harvest was gathered, he was sent to Benjamin Moore's boarding school for one year, which was divided into four quarters with 72 days each. When he came home at the end of the school year, the schoolmaster having run away and left an unfinished quarter, the boy, not yet sixteen, was asked to finish it, which he did, and also the succeeding one.

Next he went to the Gulph School, from there to Judge Jones's school-house in Lower Merion township, teaching a year in each place. The time lived in the latter was a pleasant and busy part of his life for he studied the higher branches of mathematics, under the instruction of Enoch Lewis, the celebrated mathematician. He also improved himself in English grammar. At all times Father embraced himself of an opportunity to gain a better education. He became a scholar without cost to his friends, paying back the money advanced for the year's schooling before the two years had elapsed. The wages of a country school-master, however, were so small that he gave up the business of teaching.

In his twentieth year he went to Philadelphia. He was employed first in a wholesale grocery, remaining ten weeks only, for they sold whiskey and he would not do that. Next he went into an iron store, leaving there to go into the employ of Rogers Bros., whose business was wholesale hardware and fine cutlery. They also had a large wood wharf, besides which the firm operated the iron works at Valley Forge.

His energies were all called into service in that firm. "He held a ready pen, and could post books and count figures faster than either of the brothers. At the wharf he would, if it was required, cord wood with a black man at the other end of the log, then go back to the desk and do efficient work, or perhaps be sent to do their bank business." A daughter of one of the brothers told me, "Your father was the most capable man the firm ever employed because he was a good clerk and not too proud to do all kinds of necessary work or drudgery." The death of Grandfather Woodman brought many changes, Rebecca and Henry had to return from the City, to him a real misfortune. The Rogers Brothers offered him an increase in salary, already a good one; but it was thought by the family he ought to go to the assistance of his mother, and, being a conscientious man, he thought so too. I think it was a mistaken idea of duty—Aunt Rebecca could have gotten along as well without as with him. But he brought money into the family by surveying, deed-writing, teaching, and other business of similar nature, not by farming. [This work, however, helped prepare him for the great work of writing "The History of the Valley Forge."—Ed.]

A QUAKER PREACHER

Through all the children of Edward and Sarah Woodman ran a deep current of religious thought and feeling. With Henry it was the mainspring of life, a simple religious faith, held with firm convictions, free from sectarian bias, was the influence that controlled his thought and action. He early renounced "the vanities and attractions of the world" and gave his mind to the cultivation of a religious life. During the time he resided in Philadelphia he united with the religious Society of Friends, and soon after began to speak a little in meetings for worship. About the year 1825 his gift in the ministry was acknowledged by the "people called Quakers," and he became a recommended minister of the Society. After he moved to Bucks County he experienced some trouble from such members at Wrightstown as could not understand his liberal views in religion. "Through all I have lived in that joy of soul in God and His providence, which cannot be taken away or destroyed," were his own relation of the trying events. A generous nature, a magnanimous soul, a heart with as little envy and jealousy in it as can be imagined, were my Father's natural attributes. In the social circle he delighted to please and interest all, in his household at all times very kind and indulgent, patient and loving, toward all alike.

MARRIAGE

Henry Woodman and Mary Smith, daughter of Benjamin and Mary Smith, he an elder of Wrightstown Meeting, were married on September 12, 1827, according to the order and under the care of Wrightstown monthly meeting of Friends, in the meeting-house at Wrightstown, Bucks county, Pennsylvania, May 1st, 1828, he went to reside with his wife and her aged parents.

Up to about 1840 he often visited meetings with a minute. In 1837 Mother accompanied him to Baltimore Yearly-meeting. She was not strong enough often to take such journeys. Father when preaching had a free and easy flow of language, a good clear voice, at no loss for words. Had he been educated for the pulpit, he would have been eloquent. The proudest, the richest, the poorest, and with the same truth add the wickedest folks in the neighborhood sent for Henry Woodman, when any one in the family was buried. To all he went with the same message of gospel truth and love.

Father had a fondness and good faculty for telling anecdotes. One time when in Norristown over First-day, it so happened several other cousins were in the town visiting. All were invited to take dinner at the hospitable home of Lindley and Margaret Rossitter. They lingered around the table talking of early recollections. Father told something humorous, which all enjoyed except Aunt Ruth, who straightened up, looked at him, and ejaculated: "Laws! Henry, how can thee go to meeting, preach, come back and be so shallow!" Her brother Henry was serious enough when occasion called for seriousness.

SCHOOL DIRECTOR

He was elected a member of the First Board of Directors for the public schools in Buckingham township, became the Secretary of the Board, which he continued to be, with the exception of one year, for a period of twenty-one years. The office was just suited to his unselfish nature, not one cent of money for the services in those days and very little thanks. He could work the same without either. He visited the schools often, where his genial temper rendered him a favorite with the children. He would have some exercise not usual in the school, adding a little humor with his remarks and advice. The good seed he sowed has blossomed for me through the many men and women I have met who have told me of the pleasure it gave them when he came alone into the school-room. My pleasure is in knowing that he is thus gratefully remembered by the children he so often benefitted.

"OLIVE BRANCHES"

As the years passed on in the life of Henry and Mary Woodman the little Woodmans came at intervals until seven olive branches had grown up around the parent tree. They were as follows:

Benjamin Smith Woodman, born 8th month, 22nd, 1828.

Edward Woodman, born 8th month, 19th, 1830; died aged 21 years, a young man of great promise.

Mary Smith Woodman, born 3rd month, 29th, 1833. [The only daughter and authoress of this delightful sketch of her father, still living on the homestead near Wycombe, Bucks County.]

Henry Woodman, Jr., born 8th month, 16th, 1835; died in Morrisville, Pa., on 3rd month, 7th, 1905.

William Woodman, born 7th month, 24th, 1838.

Comly Woodman, born 12th month, 30th, 1840.

Wilson Moore Woodman, born 10th month, 3rd, 1845. [His daughter, Alice Woodman Smith, being the connecting link between the Woodmans and the publisher of this book.]

THE CLOSE OF DAY

Henry and Mary Woodman continued to live on the Smith homestead in the same house fifty-two consecutive years, dating from their marriage in 1827. On Christmas eve 1879 Henry died, aged 84 years. He outlived his father fifty-seven years and was the last survivor of the Valley household. When Father was about 75 years old his mind gave evidence of failure, which gradually increased. Had it not been for an accident that occurred in 1873, he could have retained his faculties in good degree until death. An afternoon in August, when bringing the cows from pasture, the male attacked him. He recovered from his wounds, but his head was so severely injured that his mind was lost to nearly everything he had perviously known. Still much of the reverent and spiritual part of his nature remained. A friend said of him: "As he lived so he died, serving the Lord, and in his old age was not forsaken."

On the fourth day following his death after a silence at home we with a few particular friends proceeded to Wrightstown Meeting-house and found it filled with people. Elizabeth Hicks Plummer gave expression to her feeling in a beautiful sermon. When all had taken a last look of him who had lived fifty-two years in their midst, he was laid in the spot he many years before had chosen.

The Homestead

near

Wycombe, Bucks Co., Pa.

May twentieth, nineteen hundred and seven.

Aged seventy-four.

HISTORY OF VALLEY FORGE

BY HENRY WOODMAN

LETTER I

AUTHOR'S INTRODUCTION

HERE are some places in the State of Pennsylvania which ought to claim a conspicuous place in its history, as they have been rendered memorable on account of their connection with that eventful time when these colonies were contending for their freedom from foreign oppression, and which resulted in the overthrow of British authority, and the final establishment of our present free independent government. While it is admitted that there are many of sufficient notoriety to claim a place in the historian's page, there are few, if any, that have rendered themselves more worthy of this favor than the Valley Forge. Not that any splendid victories were there achieved for no engagements with the enemy took place there; the confused noise of the battle of the warrior was not heard there; neither were carnage and garments rolled in the blood of the slain beheld in its borders. But it was there that Washington with his destitute and suffering army, towards the close of the year 1777, and in one of the most gloomy seasons of the Revolution, took up his winter quarters and suffered for a period of near seven months, the most severe privations and hardships. There, but partially sheltered by miserable huts from the inclemency of a severe and protracted winter, and almost destitute of clothing and provisions, sustained by principles of the purest patriotism, they patiently endured their sufferings with true magnanimity, constancy and patient resignation, supported by the hope of ultimately obtaining the independence of their country, and enjoying the inalienable rights of men.

To preserve an account of these incidents connected with that interesting period, as well as some other matters relating to that place and the surrounding country, is the object of the present and succeeding communications. I was born and raised in the vicinity of the place, and within the lines of the encampment where many of its traces were, and still (1850) are visible; and many of the inhabitants of the neighborhood had been witnesses of that interesting and deeply trying time, from whom I received an account of the principal events that shall hereafter be noticed—

particularly those that relate to the period of the Revolution. Among those from whom this information has been derived were my parents; and it was from their lips I have heard the greater part of it. My father was a soldier during the Revolution, and was one of the number encamped there; he belonged to the North Carolina line, which constituted Washington's life guard, and was, as he informed me, in twelve general engagements. My mother, at the time of the encampment at Valley Forge, was in the nineteenth year of her age, and resided with her father, whose farm was situated within the limits of the encampment, and was the resort of numerous American officers, thus affording its inmates, from actual knowledge and observation, an intimate acquaintance of the passing events that were transpiring around them.

Often, in the days of my childhood, have I listened with deep interest to the simple unvarnished relations of that period, as they have fallen from the lips of my parents, when assembled around the fireside, of long winter evenings, sometimes in company with some of the neighbors, who had witnessed the same things; but oftener in company with strangers, and younger people, who felt desirous to hear the recital of these things, and the facts they had witnessed, related by them. Their social disposition and happy faculty of communicating these narratives rendered their company particularly interesting and agreeable. I shall never forget the time, when in early youth, I used to accompany my father and traverse the ground of the encampment, where the foundations of the huts, the fortifications and breastworks were still visible; and have heard him, while pointing out some particular objects and explaining their uses or purposes, relate the sufferings of that Spartan Band, and not only there, but during their severe struggle to accomplish our freedom. Impressions were then made upon my mind that, while reason retains her seat, I trust will never be effaced, even at that time feeling desirous that our freedom and free institutions might be perpetuated to the latest posterity, and that the evils of war might never again be found in our borders. And although I have since lived to see the inconsistency of wars and fighting with the peaceful religion of Him who emphatically declared that his "Kingdom was not of this world," yet I believe that a narration of some facts connected with that era in the Revolution, taken in contrast with our present happy, peaceable and prosperous condition, may not only be interesting but have a tendency to raise in the minds of the present generation a grateful sense of the blessings we now enjoy, and to incite them not to deeds of war or to raise a thirst for military renown, but to use every exertion on our part to preserve pure and unsullied to generations yet unborn, the inestimable blessings of peace, liberty, freedom, and self-government, which we, through the patrotism, perseverance and patient sufferings of our ancestors, are now in possession of.

What can be better calculated to call the attention of the present generation, who are now engaged in active duties of life, and also the rising youth, who, in the revolving round of a few more years, must be the future guardians of our country, than to remind them of the difficulties, dangers and hardships of various kinds that were surmounted by their predecessors in the accomplishment of our freedom, and also placing us in possession of the liberty and free system of government we now enjoy?

Actuated by motives of this nature, I have been induced to present to the public, through the medium of some of the public papers of the County of Bucks, to commence a series of letters, giving an account of Valley Forge, a place, as already mentioned, that has rendered itself conspicuous on account of its connection with the Revolutionary War; for here it was that during its darkest days, and after the successive defeats of Brandywine and Germantown and the massacre of Paoli and the possession of the City of Philadelphia by the enemy, that a part of the army, with the commander-in-chief, retired into winter quarters under the most gloomy prospects.

In presenting this series of letters to the people of my adopted county of Bucks and the public generally, it is not my intention to confine myself exclusively to the period of the Revolution, but I shall refer to the early settlement of the place and continue its history down to the present time. Neither shall I limit myself to that portion of country originally embraced in the Valley Forge tract, but shall extend the account to portions of country surrounding it in every direction, the most of which was the scene of some interesting events during the Revolution.

BEFORE THE ENCAMPMENT

LETTER II

VALLEY FORGE IN 1850

HE Valley Forge is situated on the western side of the River Schuylkill, about twenty-two miles from the city of Philadelphia, in the counties of Chester and Montgomery. The village bearing the name of Valley Forge contains (1850) about forty houses, with a large cotton factory, a grist mill, and numerous other buildings; these lie on a stream of water called the Valley Creek, which forms the dividing line between the two counties, that part lying on the eastern side being in Montgomery, and that on the western in Chester county. The water power for driving the machinery is probably not excelled by any other in Pennsylvania, as the stream passes between two abrupt hills from the fertile regions of the great valley, a distance of more than a mile, to the village, near which place these hills, or as they are more familiarly called, Mount Joy and Mount Misery, have their northern termination, at which place a large dam of more than twenty feet in height, has been constructed, which affords, in the driest seasons, a sufficiency of water to continue the manufacturing business in full operation. A public road from the city of Philadelphia to this place, called the Gulf road, originally terminated here. Another road from Phoenixville, Yellow Springs, Morgantown, Reading, and many other places, commences at the termination of the Gulf road, at the county line, and called Nutt's road, taking its name from a certain Samuel Nutt, who owned extensively at Phoenixville, in Chester county, more than a hundred years ago. Another has within a few years been laid out from the place to the Lancaster turnpike, following the course of the dam through the county of Montgomery, but as I have never travelled it, I cannot say where it terminates. About half a mile east of the village, the Gulf road is intersected by a road originally leading to the old Lancaster road, by way of the Valley Baptist Meeting House, and has been called the Baptist road, or Valley road. One thing a little remarkable is, that, though in a public place, with the Reading railroad passing through a part of the property, there has never been a hotel or tavern in the village.

As we approach the place on the eastern side by the Gulf road, as we ascend the top of the hill, a little north of the intersection of the Baptist road, the beautiful river Schuylkill bursts full upon the view, and in a line between the observer and the river, is seen the original mansion where General Washington had his headquarters during the encampment in the winter of 1777 and 78. After descending by a somewhat meandering road, we arrive at the Valley Forge, or rather the village bearing that name, the purpose of its original construction has been long since abandoned, not having been used for the manufacturing of bar iron from pigs for more than sixty years.

ORIGINAL SETTLEMENT AND THE FORGE

Concerning its original settlement I am not in the possession of any documents calculated to throw much light, or to afford correct or authentic information on the subject. I shall, therefore, rely on the accounts I have received from aged persons, all of whom have now descended to the grave—together with such facts as I have been able to collect from the old title deeds that I have had occasion to examine when engaged in surveying property contained in the original tract; but as more than twenty-two years have elapsed since that period, and the greater part of the time I have been a resident of this county (Bucks), and not having it in my power to make further investigations on this head, the information on this point will be concise and furnished only from recollection.

The original tract, containing upwards of two thousand acres, was taken by Evan ap Bevan, a native of Radnorshire, in the Principality of Wales, about the year 1686. Whether he emigrated to the country or not, I cannot say with certainty; but, from having seen his name in certain title deeds, I have come to the conclusion that he must have resided for several of the last years of his life in this, then province of Pennsylvania. One thing is certain, that he was the original ancestor of the Stephens family, since very numerous in that part of the country, and some branches of the family now in possession of a part of other lands granted to him about one hundred and sixty-four years ago. I have always understood that this was the first forge for the manufactory of iron in the Province, and was first commenced by Stephen Evans, a son of the aforesaid Evan ap Bevan (he, according to the usage and custom of the Welsh, taking his father's first name) and Lewis Walker, a son of Isaac, the original ancestor of the Walker family, since and at this time, composing a numerous and respectable portion of the inhabitants of that portion of country; some of them now being in possession of the original portion of land granted to him by the proprietor in the year 1684. Of both these families I shall have occasion to speak more fully in some of my future communications. At what time they commenced business I cannot say with certainty, but I have understood, from correct authority that, owing to some mistake between them, together with their ignorance of the business, it did not result to the advantage of the parties, and in a few years after resulted in a dissolution of the firm, and after several years of litigation, the property was sold to a certain John Potts of Burlington, in the State of New Jersey, and a large speculator in iron works in different parts of Pennsylvania.

This sale to John Potts took place about the year 1719, in whose family it remained until 1806. He was the grandfather of David and Isaac Potts, who owned the property at the time of the encampment at that place. During the time the property was owned by different members of the Potts family, nothing remarkable occurred at that time; they continued to pursue the even tenor of their way, diligently engaged in the manufactory of bar iron, and increasing in wealth and numbers, extended the business to other parts of the State. They were very patrician in their habits. They founded Pottsgrove, now Pottstown, on the Schuylkill, in the county of Montgomery, about twenty-two miles from Norristown, where many members of the family still continue to reside, pursuing their former occupations. The iron business was carried on by different members of the family at the Valley Forge, until the time of the encampment during the Revolution, when the scenes in connection with that event, and the destruction of the property attendant thereon, and the unsettled state of the country during that period, for awhile put an end to their operations.

In my next letter I shall advert to the causes that produced these effects. There are no doubt many who know of the encampment, the burning of the Valley Forge by the British, and other circumstances in relation to that, to whom details of these things may be interesting. I shall therefore endeavor to lay them before my readers in a clear and distinct manner, and as much as possible in the order of time in which they occurred, as I have often heard them related by those who had an opportunity of an experimental knowledge of these things.

they might be compared to nicely adjusted scales—the addition of a very small matter would cause one or the other to have the preponderance. Previous to the American army encamping at the place, and while the possession of the city of Philadelphia, during the ensuing winter, by either party was uncertain, the Valley Forge was selected as a suitable place for the depository of the military stores, arms and ammunition, and the provisions belonging to the continental army. The selection was made on account of its secluded situation and distance from the supposed route of the British army under Gen. Howe, in its march from the Chesapeake Bay, to form a junction with Gen. Burgoyne, who with the army under his command, were on their route from Canada by way of the Lakes, to get possession of the city of Philadelphia in their march; and, as it was also believed by many, that they had this place in view for winter quarters, in case the enemy succeeded in getting possession of the city of Philadelphia, believing the inhabitants in that section of country, were less loyal than in some other places, and that they generally favored the American cause.

However correct this last position may have been in general, and however patriotic the most of them might have been; yet from this there were some exceptions. It must be acknowledged that there were some, though not in the immediate vicinity of the place, or residing in that portion of the country which I mean particularly to describe—ready to convey the information to the enemy; and one, if not more, who acted as a pilot to conduct a detachment of the British army to the place, who succeeded in destroying the most of the buildings belonging to the manufacturing establishment, and such part of the stores, arms, ammunitions, and provisions, as had not been hastily removed to the opposite side of the river Schuylkill.

At the time of the conflagration, the manufacturing of iron at the place was carried on by a person, who will occupy a conspicuous place in this account, named William Dewees, in connection with some members of the Potts family. Whether he at this time owned any part of the real estate or not, I cannot say. He was then married to his second wife, his former one having been a Potts; but whether or not a sister of Isaac and David Potts, mentioned in my last letter, I have never fully informed myself. It was in part owing to this marriage connection that William Dewees, in his life time, founded a claim on government, for damages for losses sustained by the burning of Valley Forge, by the British; and about nine years after his death, was successfully prosecuted by his widow and some of his heirs; which I merely hint at here, as I shall probably enter more into its details in some future communications. His second wife was the daughter of a wealthy and respectable inhabitant, named Thomas

Waters, residing in the Great Valley, about two miles east of the place—of whom some notice will be taken hereafter.

William Dewees was at the time a colonel of the Continental militia, and served a campaign in the field during the war of the Revolution. Owing to the commission and rank he held in the army, he was rendered particularly obnoxious to the enemy; and they, of course, resorted to every means in their power to harass and, if possible, to take him prisoner. On this account the place of depository for the military stores at Valley Forge was strongly opposed by Col. Dewees (as he will henceforth be called) and his wife, they being almost certain that the buildings would be destroyed, on account of his connection with the army, and of course, it could not be a safe depository for them. The sequel proved the soundness of their views. In my next I shall resume the subject.

LETTER IV

THE BURNING OF THE VALLEY FORGE

DO NOT know the precise date of the burning of the Valley Forge, but it occurred during the interval of time between the battles of Brandywine and Germantown, and but a short time previous to the massacre at the Paoli. My mother, though not an eye witness to the scene or conflagration, was placed in a situation on that day which made her a prominent character on the occasion. She had been on a perilous embassy, which having accomplished, on her return home, had to pass the place on that day, and but a short time previous to the perpetration of the deed. Having in passing the place, beheld the hurry, bustle and confusion attendant upon the removal of the stores belonging to the army to the other side of the river, she often used to relate it; and from this information I shall now proceed to insert it here. I consider the circumstances of this journey of sufficient interest to claim a place in this narrative, as they will show the present generation, now lolling in ease and enjoyment, the difficulties that had then to be, through necessity, encountered often by tender and delicate females, and through how much they sometimes persevered, in order to overcome them.

HUNTING JEHU—TWO WOMEN OF THE REVOLUTION

It has been observed that the Valley Forge was burned between the battles of Brandywine and Germantown. Soon after the battle of Brandywine, the sick and wounded were for a short time conveyed to Philadelphia, and the American army under Washington, was marched to Skippack, in the county of Montgomery. General Howe, with that part of the British army under his command, encamped for a few days at the house of Samuel Richards, in the great valley, about three miles southeast of the Valley Forge. Kniphausen, who had the command of the Hessians, had his quarters at the house of a respectable German named Jacob Fricke, on the adjoining farm. The Hessians during their stay at the place were troublesome neighbors. They committed many depredations and thefts—entering with impunity into houses, taking everything valuable they could lay their hands on, often jeopardizing the lives, and spreading dismay among the peaceable inhabitants, and rendering traveling dangerous and almost impracticable.

LETTER V

T THE conclusion of my last letter, our travelers were about resuming their homeward journey. When ready to leave the Falls of Schuylkill, the day was far spent, and they had proceeded but a little way when night overtook them, and it commenced raining. Proceeding up the Ridge Road, not being able to cross the river, they concluded to continue to Archibald Thomson's, about a mile above where Norristown now stands. At that time there was no town there; the only house on the present site of the town, was that of John Bull, who owned the greater part of the land on which Norristown is now built. This house was near Stony Creek bridge, in the upper end of the town; the next house below, was immediately opposite the old Swedes Ford, more than a mile distant. The town now (1850) contains more than seven thousand inhabitants—such has been the rapid increase and march of improvement since that period. They kept on their journey through the rain. When they arrived at Thomson's, they found the house empty, with the exception of a black man, who was left to take care of the premises. Thomson being an officer in the army, fled with his family for fear of the British, who, in a few days after, burned the buildings on his place, and also the barn of John Bull on Stony Creek; although his name partook of royalty, he was in principle opposed to it, being a staunch Republican.

Not thinking it safe to continue there, and not finding quarters as expected, they proceeded on to Henry Pawling's, at Pawling's Ford, on the Schuylkill, about six miles farther up, where they arrived about midnight. Riding up to the house, my mother called out to some of the inmates to arise; her voice was heard and recognized by Nathan Pawling (afterwards sheriff of Montgomery county), who, alarmed at her arriving there at that time of the night, hastily cried out, "What is the matter, Sarah, that you come here at this time of night?" She told him to arise, let them in, and take care of their horses, and she would let him know. This request was soon willingly complied with; and, other members of the family arising, they were soon comfortably supplied with such things as they stood in need of, in their tired situation.

Here they learned the disturbed state of things at Valley Forge, which was situate on the opposite side of the river, and from which place they were then removing the stores on temporary rafts, constructed for the purpose, as expeditiously as possible, across the river, expecting an immediate attack from the enemy; this caused much fear and consternation among the people, and may account for the surprise occasioned by the arrival of two females at midnight, from the opposite side of the river, and from the scene of confusion and fear.

The following morning the rain had ceased and the weather was clear and serene; but all was hurry and confusion, occasioned by removing property from Valley Forge. Upon one of the rafts constructed for the occasion, they were ferried over and safely landed on their own side of the water, not more than two miles from home. Soon after they crossed over, they saw Col. Dewees hurrying to cross over the river, momentarily expecting the enemy; and Col. Lee, who was stationed here to guard the stores, in company with Col. Hamilton, busily engaged in moving them away.

Passing on their journey towards home, near the foot of the hill mentioned in my second letter, at the junction of the Gulf and Baptist roads, [where the old school-house stands—Ed.] hearing a noise in the woods on their right, my mother looking in that direction, saw coming toward them a body of British cavalry, moving in the most perfect order, their horses being so trained that they made but little noise in their march. In their front, in company with an officer, rode a guide or pilot, whom she knew, but who shall in this description be nameless; one who, if report be true, was often engaged in similar expeditions during the war. They passed on without noticing or molesting them, except that an officer left his station, rode up to them, and inquired of them whether they had been at Valley Forge and seen Col. Dewees? and whether they were removing the military stores? Receiving from her an affirmative answer, he took his leave and resumed his station in the company, who proceeded on to the river, but not by the direct road, and found Col. Dewees on a raft, crossing over to the other side of the river. They fired upon him, killed the Colonel's horse, but did no further injury to any of the company. Cols. Lee and Hamilton each made a hasty retreat from the place, in different directions; and the men engaged on the occasion precipitately fled from the enemy when they saw them approaching. Some carbines were fired after them, but none took any effect. The place being thus left to the mercy of the enemy, they set fire to the buildings in which the stores were deposited, the forge and all the buildings appertaining to it, all of which with their contents were destroyed.

While these things were in progress at Valley Forge, our travelers arrived safely at home, fondly hoping that their perils were at an end. But this hope was short lived, for in a few minutes after their arrival, three Hessians armed with daggers, were seen approaching the house, which they soon entered, and began to plunder of whatever valuable things they could lay hold of. In my next, I shall give a detail of this unceremonious visit. In the residue of this I shall confine myself to such matters as relate (as my mother called it) to her journey "to hunt Jehu."

One of the Hessians saw their saddles, which, upon being taken off the horses, were placed in the sun to dry. He inquired in broken English, whose they were; she replied, "Mine." He then drew his dagger and exclaimed in a rage, as nearly as could be understood: "You rebel, you have been to see Washington!" but offered no further signs of violence. Some little time after they withdrew, she heard the sound of military music, and looking in the direction from whence it came, saw a large number of British soldiers approaching the house. When they came opposite, they made a halt, and an officer came to her and inquired whether Thomas Waters lived there; she said, "No." His next inquiry was where he lived; she pointed to the place, it being the next farm. He then asked if she would sell him a loaf of bread; she told him she would, and then brought him one. "Look at me," said he, "that you may know me again. After we go to Thomas Waters's, we will come back, and I will pay you. We expect to encamp there for the night, and return this way." He then joined the company, who proceeded on their march; but he never came back to pay for the loaf of bread; and she, with the rest of the family, were glad to escape with no greater loss.

Thus ended the four eventful days of my mother's journey to hunt Jehu. To some these things may seem a fiction; but it is nevertheless an unvarnished truth; and there are now living in the borough of Doylestown several persons of respectability who have heard her relate the circumstances mentioned in this narrative, particularly the account of her journey.

It may not be improper to state in this place, in relation to the burning of the Valley Forge, Colonel Caleb North, since Sheriff of the city and county of Philadelphia, informed me thirty-nine years after the event, that he saw the conflagration from the top of Mt. Joy, near the place. He, in company with Colonel Alexander Hamilton, had been sent to the place—Hamilton to join Lee in the removal of the stores, and he, to watch incognito the movements of the British army in the neighborhood.

In my next I shall give an account more fully of the Hessians' visit to my grandfather's, and the sequel of the march of the British to Thomas Waters's, who was marked as one of their objects of persecution, on account of his being father-in-law to Colonel Dewees, whose family were at this time at the place.

Quarters of Wheedon and of DeKalb

home of Abijah Stephens, original house razed and present built by Stephens in 1811 and recently improved by Commissioner John R. K. Scott as his summer residence. See pages 49, 57-58, 66-67, 71-72, 121-122.

The birthplace of the author, Henry Woodman. Now the home of Wm. Foterall, on the south side of Trout Creek, on the road from Port Kennedy to King-of-Prussia. See pages 19 and 163-164.

Old School House built by Letitia Penn in 1705 and occupied by the Continental Army as a Hospital during the Winter of 1777-1778. Repaired 1907. Valley Forge Park, Pa.

Interior of the Old Camp School House. Here the author attended school, and from here his History of Valley Forge goes forth.

LETTER VI

UNCEREMONIOUS VISIT OF THE HESSIANS

AVING promised my readers to give a more full detail of the unceremonious visit of the Hessians to my grandfather's family, I now enter upon that duty. When they saw them coming to the house, there were several men sitting on seats at the front door, enough at least, to have prevented their doing much damage; but thinking self-preservation the first law of nature, they all fled in different directions, except my grandfather and his only son, the late Stephen Stephens, deceased between four and five years since, a man since well known to many persons in this county, a lad then about thirteen years of age. They sat still to abide the consequences that might befall them. Among those who fled for safety was a chaplain to the American army, belonging to Mifflin's division, named William Rogers, a Baptist clergyman, and afterwards, for many years, professor of rhetoric and belles-letters in the University of Pennsylvania. Knowing that his dress would betray him as belonging to the army, he ran into the house, handed my mother his coat and a valuable gold watch to take care of until he should come back, then ran and hid himself under an open ended hogshead in the cellar (as he many years after informed me). She took the watch and hastened with it up stairs, locked it in a drawer, and took the coat to a bunch of bushes near the house, and hid it among them.

When the Hessians arrived, one of them seized my grandfather by the collar, drew his dagger, and robbed him of a watch that was in his pocket, and then proceeded into the house. His mother, an old woman, and who from a paralytic stroke was completely prostrated, both in mind and body, and totally incapable of helping herself, sat tied in an arm chair (one that I think is still in possession of our family).

However disposed to treat other members of the family, if not with rudeness, it was far from civility and politeness; they each, as they passed her, took her affectionately by the hand, and in their broken language called her mother, and appeared to reverence old age. They next proceeded upstairs, and commenced breaking open the drawers and cupboards, rifling them of their contents, and taking whatever they considered of sufficient value to carry off. The first thing of value that attracted their attention was the chaplain's gold watch, which they secured and carried off in triumph. His coat remained unobserved in the bushes, and so might his watch if it had been placed in one of the pockets and hid with it, or have been left by him, as he was not discovered.

Among other things found in ransacking the drawers were a number of cartridges, that had been found by the lad above mentioned, a few days before, and placed in the drawer, without suspecting any evil consequences would arise from this simple circumstance. Finding these so enraged the plunderers, who suspected from this trifling affair that they were connected with the army, that they became so turbulent that fears for their safety were strongly apprehended, the family believing they would proceed to violent measures. Some explanation being made, and finding nothing further to confirm their suspicions they soon became quiet and offered no further violence to any.

Having seen the respect they paid to the aged woman before mentioned, some of the family availed themselves of the opportunity, while the Hessians were upstairs, of placing in her pockets some silver spoons and other small articles of value, and owing to this circumstance they escaped their notice. It was well that she did not understand their language or comprehend their meaning, otherwise she would, owing to her dotage, by her words and actions, expressive of her anxiety, have betrayed the secret of their being secreted about her person. After taking whatever they thought proper, and among other things the articles (consisting principally of groceries), which my mother had purchased during her late expedition, they departed from the house.

Crossing over a small stream of water they found sitting, under a large walnut tree an old man, a brother of my grandfather, generally known by the name of Uncle Benjamin, engaged in shaving splints to make baskets, and who had not been apprised of what was passing in the house. Coming up to him they demanded of him whether he was a rebel man, an epithet very familiar with them. They received from him a very cool reception and abrupt answer, for being armed with a sharp axe, and furnished with several pieces of white oak wood for making splints, about eight feet long, and split into pieces of sufficient lightness to handle with ease, he did not fear them. Instead of answering them, he told them to clear out, or (to use his own expression) he would brain some of them, at the same time making use of actions suitable to the words. They soon left him, either thinking him an object not worthy of their notice, or fearing a stroke from his axe. It was probably well that they desisted, as he was of a very vindictive spirit and given to broils and fighting, and he might, in all probability, have carried his threats into execution.

They next proceeded to Thomas Waters's, and having plundered the house of many valuable things, took a notion to feast upon some fowls. While in pursuit of them, some ran under an old smoke-house, where one of the pursuers followed them. Whether he succeeded in capturing any fowls or not, tradition does not inform us, but they succeeded in finding something of more value,—a large sum of money, in coin, had been secreted there to prevent its falling into the hands of the enemy. Having succeeded so well, they proceeded to their camp, stopping at the next farm above, and carrying from a tree some green persimmons, a fruit at the time not very palatable to them.

There is a circumstance connected with this account, I will next mention here. The large walnut tree alluded to is still standing (1850), a few venerable elms, that escaped the ravages of that period, are the only relics of the Revolution that I know of that now remain on my grandfather's property.

PHIN'S FORT

Neither can I close this account without introducing to the notice of my readers, one, who at the time of the visit of the Hessians, rendered himself of some notoriety. I allude to a black man, a slave of my grandfather, named Phineas, generally called "Phin," for be it known that at the time slavery existed in Pennsylvania, and Friends, of whom my grandfather was one, as well as others, held them in unconditional servitude. Phin, seeing the Hessians coming, ran into the house, took down a long gun, which is still in possession of some of the family, and hastily seizing some of the ammunition, ran some distance to a sinking hole or cave, where he hid himself for several days, coming home at night for food; and, as he said, determined to defend himself from the enemy. The place of his retreat was afterwards called by my father, "Phin's Fort," a name it still retains and may possibly for some years to come.

The detachment of British soldiers, mentioned in my last, proceeded to the farm of Thomas Waters, took off a large quantity of hay, grain, and many other articles, drove off some cattle and horses, and then returned the same night to their camp. This was the last time that any of the British or Hessians were on my grandfather's property in a hostile manner.

In my next I shall, in addition to some things growing out of the events mentioned in this letter, make some general remarks, on the state of the times, and some other matters, which I trust will be of interest to my readers.

LETTER VII

GENERAL OBSERVATIONS

T MUST appear evident from the foregoing accounts, that these were truly troublesome times. As noticed in one of my former letters, parties were nearly balanced. And there were others who wished to assume a neutral position. The latter though not so much persecuted by the contending parties, were subjected to requisitions from both armies, and found their situation at best a very critical one, as much caution was necessary to preserve a strict neutrality, the movements of all were strictly watched. Those who adhered to the crown were persecuted by the colonists and the colonial army; and those who were known to be opposed to British authority, and openly acknowledged themselves in favor of freedom, and especially those who held commissions in the army, or were active in the service of the Continental Congress, were marked as the objects of revenge by the enemy; while those who held a neutral position, and were not active in the cause of freedom, however they might be secretly disposed to favor it, if when requisitions for the use of either army were made upon them, or their houses were entered by the British soldiery, if nothing was found in their possession that would have a tendency to convict them of any of the rebellious movements of that day, they were seldom much molested. But if anything, however small, was found in their houses, or in their possession, it was often the cause of violence on the part of the enemy. This may account for the rage of the Hessians, upon finding the cartridges, as before noticed, in possession of my grandfather; and had they upon that occasion discovered anything else indicative of a hostile nature, or intended for hostile purposes, their resentment might possibly have known no bounds; and serious, if not fatal consequences might have followed.

DEWEE'S REGALIA

The family was at this time in imminent danger, though entirely ignorant of it. The circumstances were these: The family of Colonel Dewees had left Valley Forge, and with the most of their furniture, had removed to his father-in-law's (Thomas Waters'), where his wife and family, for the time being professing to be strict loyalists, were staying. Among the articles of furniture removed from Valley Forge were two chests which the wife of the Colonel wished to have kept at my grandfather's, she assuring them they contained nothing but some articles of clothing and some other things, which she wished to have secured in case of the enemy coming upon them. My grandmother, all kindness, consented to the request, and they were brought there. When the Hessians visited the house, although the chests were in the house and in one of the rooms they plundered, yet they were not broken open. Feeling uneasy on account of not knowing what was in them, on the following day, my mother went to Sarah Dewees, wife of the Colonel, and requested, or rather demanded the keys, that she might with certainty know what was contained in them; she told her to make herself perfectly easy, as there was nothing in them that if discovered would hurt or injure them. Being peremptory in her demand, the keys were reluctantly delivered to her, and she proceeded to open the chests, and to her surprise, found they contained the Colonel's military uniform and insignias of office, his sword and other weapons worn by officers of his rank, which if they had been discovered, would have produced much destruction of property, if not loss of life. She immediately gathered the whole contents into her arms, carried them to a quarry in a coppice of woods near the house (the place can now be pointed out), in which she threw the whole of them, and covering them with stones,—thus spoiled the Colonel's hat and other military accoutrements. By this disinterested act of kindness, we may observe how narrowly they escaped the dangers to which they were unsuspectingly subjected, and the imminent danger they were placed in.

It may be proper to remark in justice to the commander of the British army, whose policy it was to secure as much as possible the confidence of the people, that these petty robberies and depredations were not sanctioned by him, or committed under his direction. They were done by a few Hessians who strolled from the camp, and committed these acts on their own responsibility. My grandfather's family was not a solitary instance of suffering from their rapacity. In their predatory movements, at the time alluded to, they paid no respect to persons, but visited all families, and treated all in the same unwelcome manner, taking everything of value they could lay hands upon and were able to carry off, so there were few, if any families, but suffered in a greater or less degree, from their approximity to them. In some cases they were followed to the camp, and upon being pointed out to the superior officers, they were punished and as far as possible restoration made of the property. But few people in the neighborhood availed themselves of that method; for though the most of them, on account of their religious principles, had assumed a neutral position, yet there were few, if any, but who were heartily disposed to favor the cause of freedom, and opposed to the royalist cause; and when the British army took from the people who were known to be neither directly or indirectly concerned with the opposing party, any articles that were not necessary to the support of their troops, restitution was always promptly made. Not as was generally supposed, so much from a sense of honesty, as a desire to secure from such conduct, the attachment and loyalty of the people.

HOWE AND BURGOYNE

The American army having abandoned the city of Philadelphia, and removed their sick and wounded, the British under command of Gen. Howe, took possession of it. The battle of Germantown took place soon after, the result of which is too well known to be repeated here—suffice it to say, that in that engagement Gen. Nash was slain. It was to his division my father belonged; he was intimately acquainted with the General in Hillsborough, North Carolina, where they both resided previous to the war, and always spoke of him in terms of the highest respect. He was near him when he fell, and was among the few others who conveyed his lifeless body to the cemetery of Towamencin Church, in Montgomery, where it is interred, and where I have understood a monument has been erected to his memory. It was near this place, on the heights of the Perkiomen and Skippack, called the Mathachen Hills, that Washington with his army retired after the engagements, to recruit his forlorn and distressed soldiers, many of whom were almost ready to give up the cause of freedom as hopeless.

In my next I shall resume the subject and endeavor to bring it up to the time of the arrival of the army at Valley Forge.

LETTER VIII

T THE close of my last, we left Washington with his troops encamped on the Mathachen Hills, to which place he had retreated to recruit, as far as possibly remained in his power, the strength and spirits of his destitute and suffering army. After tarrying here a few days and receiving some reinforcements, he marched back again towards Philadelphia, to watch the movements of the enemy, and encamped on the heights of Barren Hill, in the township of Whitemarsh, and the Gulf Hills, in Upper Merion township, Montgomery county—a portion being on both sides of the river Schuylkill. The British fleet was at this time trying to force a passage up the Delaware to the city of Philadelphia, which after six weeks of fierce and determined opposition, they finally effected. While here several small skirmishes took place, but no decisive battles were fought. And it was also while encamped here that too important matters took place, which I shall now advert to.

The first was the welcome news of the capture of General Burgoyne and his army by General Gates, in the state of New York. This news had the tendency to raise the drooping spirits of the desponding army, though gloomy the prospect and trying the condition in which they were placed to hold on and persevere in the cause of freedom and independence, under their severe sufferings and hardships. Previous to this news reaching them, many of them who were persons of wealth and respectability who had exchanged their comfortable homes, their happy firesides, and their plentiful tables, for the toils, hardships and deprivations of a camp and the life of a soldier; and seeing for a time at least nothing but defeats and disasters attend them, were almost ready to throw down their arms and reluctantly give up the cause of freedom as hopeless, now felt a ray of hope. Animated by it, and like a drowning man grasping at a straw to prolong his existence, so they seized on the news of that victory as a fresh stimulus, to excite them to contend for their freedom, looking forward through the dark and gloomy prospect of that day to a brighter and better day, and afresh resolved to still hold on in sustaining the ground they had taken.

LYDIA DARRACH AND ANOTHER FEMALE

The other event alluded to was the discovery of a plan of the British army to surprise and capture the army under Washington, while stationed at these places. The plan was frustrated by the vigilance, sagacity, and I may add, patriotism of a woman in the city of Philadelphia, named Lydia Darrach, a member of the Society of Friends, at whose house the British officers had a room in which they met to hold private consultations. On one occasion of this kind she overheard a plan of arrangement laid down, and the time agreed upon, to make an attack on the whole army and take them by surprise. This by a well concerted stratagem on her part, which shows how fertile the female mind often is in cases of emergency and difficulties to be overcome, to devise the means necessary to carry them into effect. The information was communicated to Washington and their object defeated.

These two causes accelerated the removal of the Continental troops to Valley Forge. The first inspired them with hope, the second showed them the necessity of being further removed from the enemy, and being fortified in case of an attack.

Having noticed the ingenuity of the female mind, and how fertile they sometimes are in carrying out any objects they have in view, even under very disadvantageous circumstances, I may be excused if I deviate a little from my subject and locality to relate a circumstance of the kind, which was planned and executed by a female who some years afterward removed to live within the limits of the lines of the encampment at Valley Forge, and on that account I give it a place here, though the object she had in view was in direct opposition to the interests of the colony. The facts I have heard her relate, and it is from that authority that I insert them, though names will be omitted, as there are some of their descendants living in an adjoining county, who, if willing that the accout should be published, would be unwilling to see the names of the persons accompany it. The circumstances occurred soon after the British took possession of Philadelphia, and are as nearly as follows:

There lived at that time in York county in this state, a man of wealth and influence, who took an active and decided part with the enemy. Owing to his known adherence and open avowal of his attachment to the royal cause, he was arrested by the Colonial authority, and confined in the prison at York, to await a trial for aiding and abetting the enemy. On account of his wealth and standing he was, though confined to the house, allowed to have full liberty of the yard, and to have rooms furnished so that he could receive and entertain company who visited him. On a certain evening he had made an entertainment, to which he had invited the Sheriff and the principal inhabitants of the town, and, it was said, some members of Congress, who were in session at the place. A splendid supper was provided for them, and plenty of wine and other liquors to drink. While the company was engaged eating and drinking, his wife, the woman last alluded to, was on the outside of the wall, preparing to effect his escape, by a plan very systematically arranged between them and successfully carried into effect.

She had prepared a rope to be thrown over the wall to him; she by holding the other end was to enable him to scale the wall. If he succeeded, two fleet horses were in readiness for them to mount and ride off with all expedition they possibly could. The company being engaged as above mentioned, he suddenly complained of indisposition, asked the company to excuse him for a short time, and leaving his hat on the table to avoid suspicion, he walked into the yard. Reaching the place, he found the rope provided too short. She immediately mounted her horse, which enabled him to reach the end of it, so that he thereby made his escape over the wall, where a hat and change of raiment were in readiness for him. They then set off at full speed to a point on the Susquehanna river, not on the main road, where arrangements had been made to cross over the river, leave the horses, and pursue their journey on others that were to be in readiness on the other side. He was soon missed, finding he had escaped, pursuit was soon commenced, but owing to her well arranged plans, they soon crossed over the river and continued their journey so expeditiously that on the morning of the following day they arrived at a house about three miles from Valley Forge, where, thirty-six years after, she ended a useful and exemplary life in a good old age.

They continued there during the day, and in the evening left the place to pursue their journey to join the British in Philadelphia, leaving the place so as to reach the city by daylight. As they drew near the city they found themselves closely pursued, when, to prevent being taken, they separated. He then rode into the river, swam his horse across and escaped to the British, where she having found means to cross the river, soon joined him.

Whether the sheriff of York county was secretly in favor of the measure or not, is uncertain, and must always remain so. And whether the owner of the house, where they stopped during the day, was previously acquainted with the movement and disposed to favor it, have been a matter of conjecture among the people of the neighborhood, and different sentiments have been entertained concerning the subject, some exculpating him from any participation in the matter, while others have considered him censurable and disposed to favor the enemy. I had prepared some comments on the subject, but have concluded not to insert them in this work; merely stating that after the war his devotion to our free institutions and tenacity, notwithstanding his religious opinions, in exercising his right of suffrage during a long period of years, warrants me in uniting with the former opinion, and shall now dismiss the subject.

Having now completed the principal matters relative to the burning of Valley Forge and other subjects that transpired about that time, I shall in my next give some account of the arrival of the troops in the vicinity of the place, from recollection of the relations that have been given me by those who were witnessess of the painful scene, principally from members of our own family whose lot it was to reside within the lines of the army during the whole period of its encampment at that place, suffering more than can be described, but which I leave to the imagination of the reader to conceive and contrast it with our present happy situation of ease and enjoyment.

And before I conclude, I would just observe that in my next the account will be generally confined to the arrival of the soldiers at my grandfather's, and their situation at the time. And whatever may be related respecting them, may be taken as applicable to other families in the neighborhood, as they all suffered alike during that disastrous time. To enter into particulars would exceed the object in view. I have therefore his family taken as a specimen, from being better acquainted with matters that occurred here at the time.

The March to Valley Forge

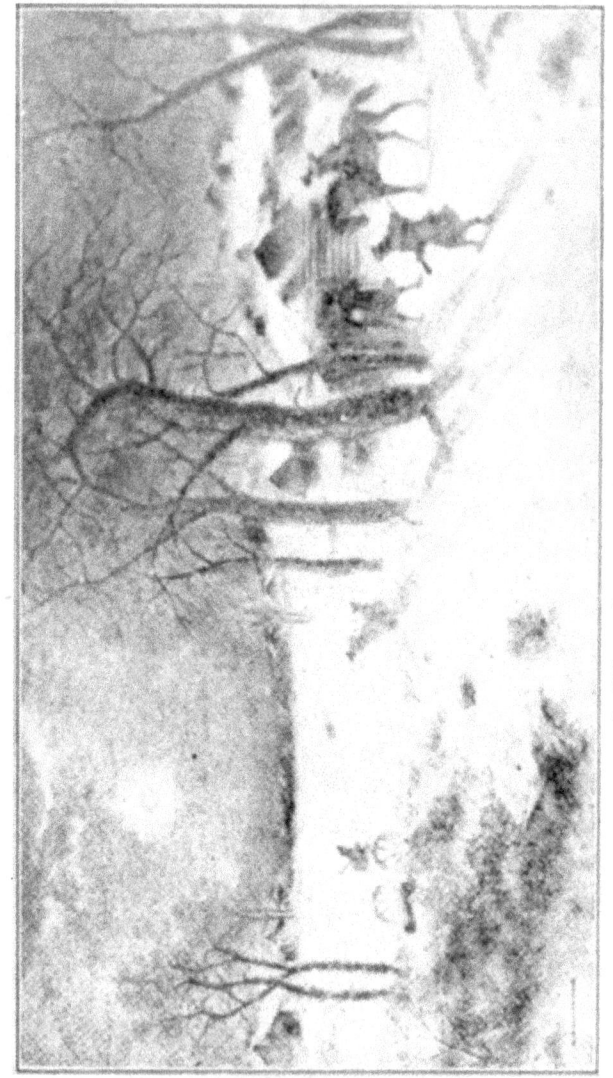

In Winter Quarters at Valley Forge

THE ENCAMPMENT PROPER

LETTER IX

ARRIVAL OF THE ARMY

IT WAS in the latter part of the year 1777 (Dec. 19), and about six weeks after the battle of Germantown, that the American army, under command of Washington, encamped for the winter at Valley Forge.

The people of the neighborhood had but little notice given them of the intention of the army encamping there, previous to their arrival at the place. Necessity obliged the officers to use much secrecy and to be cautious in all their movements, particularly at this critical time, when the people were under a general depression, and the soldiers nearly destitute of food and clothing and other necessaries, and more than two thousand of them had been marched bare-footed from one place to another, often through frost and snow, leaving the ground over which they marched marked with blood, to evade an attack from the enemy. At the same time, disheartened and dispirited from successive defeats, and almost worn down with fatigue, in their frequent marches to keep out of the way of their powerful enemy, who, through their emissaries, were mostly apprized of their movements, and were on the alert to secure the most favorable opportunity to crush them at a blow, and reduce the colonies to subjection.

Under circumstances of this nature, it was essentially necessary that all their movements should be conducted with caution and secrecy. This may account for little or no notice being given to the inhabitants of the neighborhood, until the officers who preceded the main body of the army to provide quarters for the general officers, on the morning of the day of their movement to the place, arrived at different houses in the vicinity and designated their particular quarters. This gave the inhabitants at whose houses the different officers were to be quartered, but very little time to prepare for their reception.

On that morning, as I have often heard my mother and others of the family relate the circumstances, an officer arrived at their house, and, without further ceremony, wrote upon the door "GENERAL WHEEDON'S QUARTERS," and then informed them that the General with his guard would arrive there during the day. Upon receiving this notice, they began to prepare to receive their visitors.

Knowing the destitute and suffering state of the army and the hardships the soldiers had to pass through, my grandmother, who possessed a disposition of the most universal benevolence to the whole family; and, however opposed she was to the system of war and bloodshed and the evils attendant upon them, yet, she could view the soldiers in no other light than fellow beings, suffering all the united calamities of hunger, cold, fatigue and sickness, and her philanthropic mind influenced by a desire to mitigate as far as possible their sufferings, began immediately to make preparations to provide something for them to eat upon their arrival. They had that season secured a large crop of buckwheat and had in the house at the time a great abundance of meal that had been manufactured from it, and but a few days previous killed a beef. They were, therefore, in some ways, prepared to receive them. They immediately prepared a large tub-full of buckwheat batter, and when sufficiently leavened, they commenced baking cakes, to be in readiness when the soldiers arrived, and, at the same time, put all their iron pots, of all sorts and sizes into requisition to boil scraps, shins and other pieces of beef, to make a large quantity of soup or broth for them.

Before proceeding further with this narrative, it may not be improper to take some notice in this place of Gen. Joseph Wheedon, whose quarters were at my grandfather's. Holding, as he did, the rank of a major general, it is somewhat remarkable that little or no notice has ever been taken of him in any of the accounts of the Revolution or in American biography. I have no recollection of ever seeing his name in print, and had it not been for the fact of his being quartered there, his name, as regards myself and many of my readers, might have long since sunk in oblivion. Some may, therefore, feel a desire to know who he was. All I can say concerning him is from recollection of what I have heard from my parents and others who had an opportunity of knowing him at that time. His residence was in Nansemond county, in Virginia, where, before the war, he kept what was called in that country an ordinary, that is, in our phrase, a tavern of an inferior kind. It was said of him, while in that capacity, that the drinking utensils of his bar were made of gourds; whether this story is correct or not I am not able to say; but it is certain that he was dubbed Joe Gourd by the officers and soldiers under him during his abode at my grandfather's, a name that he was called by for many years afterward, and not entirely abandoned at the present time, as I have heard it given him but a few weeks since, by an aged woman of the family, who well remembers his being at the house at the time alluded to above.

He was of a very haughty and arrogant disposition, and treated the soldiers under him with the utmost cruelty and tyranny, viewing them more in the capacity of his negro slaves, over

The History of Valley Forge 51

whom he was privileged to exercise the most despotic authority, than the brave advocates of freedom, struggling in the cause of obtaining their liberty, and patiently striving to surmount the most formidable objects that opposed their progress in the attainment of it. By the accounts I have heard of him
"The milk of human kindness never warmed his breast."
He may, therefore, be held up to view as one raised to greatness without merit, and show the abuse such make of their power when dressed with a little brief authority, or deputed to exercise the command of others. While his authority over those under his command was not only duly but rigidly enforced to keep them in abject subjection and pay servile homage to his person, he never exercised it to prevent them from taking from the family and others, anything they could lay their hands upon; and, if he did not encourage such acts, he never, as I have understood, endeavored in the least degree to discourage them, or interposed to prevent it. I shall notice him further in some subsequent communication.

But to proceed to my narrative. The cakes being baked and the soup got in readiness and well thickened with buckwheat cakes and vegetables, the soldiers soon after began to arrive in a truly deplorable condition; and as regards their clothing, appearance and distress, it need not be repeated. Almost famished with hunger, they soon began like ravenous animals to devour the food provided for them. Before they had finished their meal, the General and suite arrived, and his first introduction was a haughty display of his imperious temper, in driving the poor, fatigued, and famished men out of the house, striking some of them with his sword, using the most blasphemous language, calling them impious names for entering the house, and daring to eat before his arrival, and uttering oaths not to be repeated; and such was their terror and fear of him, that they fled from his presence as from a dangerous pestilence, or the fury of a lion.

This cruel treatment was more than my worthy grandmother could tolerate; for though of the most pacific disposition, and endued with a heart of tenderness and compassion towards the meanest insect, yet where suffering humanity was concerned, and it was in her power to administer to its relief, she had not only a firmness of spirit, but a firmness of resolution to carry her motives into effect. Unintimidated by the General's supercilious behavior and regardless of his threats, she resolutely commanded some of the soldiers to return and carry out a large iron pot, which is still in possession of our family, and several smaller ones that were well filled with soup, and furnishing them with an additional supply of cakes, that had been previously prepared for the occasion, they did so, and soon devoured their contents, they not being quite so fastidious as some of our modern epicures. Often have I heard my aged grandmother describe the events of that day; and always on these occasions her eyes would fill with tears, in recollecting the distressed situation of the soldiers upon their arrival, and describing as she was accustomed to do, the contemptible behavior of the General toward them, not only on that day, but almost every day during the time he had his quarters at their house, though he was there but a short time.

From what information I have been able to gather, the soldiers upon arriving at their respective quarters, were in the same famished condition, and they were also provided for in a similar manner; but I never heard of any being treated in the same cruel manner that Wheedon treated his men, as related in the foregoing account.

I shall now close the communication by just informing my readers, that in my next I shall give some account of the location of the encampment, and the situation of the surrounding country, the erection of fortifications, huts and breast works, and other things relating to the commencement of the encampment.

In describing places on the river Schuylkill, the eastern and western sides of the river are made use of, without regarding the source at the particular places; its course is so devious as often to present a very contrary appearance. The city of Philadelphia is on its eastern side, and all places mentioned on that side of the river are given on the eastern side, and those on the opposite side, on the western.

LETTER X

LOCATING THE ENCAMPMENT

THE location of the encampment of the main body of the army was on an eminence lying on the western side of the river Schuylkill, commencing on the farm then belonging to Mordecai Moore, the father of Jesse Moore, who was for many years Presiding Judge of the Sixth Judicial District of Pennsylvaina, and extending from thence in a south-westwardly direction, having the front line of the encampment on the first elevation of the north valley hill, and since called the Front Line Hill, more than two miles, and terminating on the farm of John Brown near the Valley Creek, in Chester County, the greater part of the ground occupied for the purpose, being in the then county of Philadelphia, now Montgomery. In order to protect themselves from an attack from the enemy, they erected at the northern extremities of the encampment, two forts, one on the land of Mordecai Moore, the other about forty rods distant, on the land of John Moore. The remains of them are still sufficiently visible to point out their size and situation, and to show the observer the uses for which they were intended. I shall speak more fully of them in some of my future letters, just mentioning in this place, that in my early days, and as long as I can remember, these were called Mordecai Moore Fort and John Moore's Fort; and as they still retain these names, they will in future references to them, be thus designated. From the first mentioned fort they threw up a breast work, running from thence on the Front Line Hill, nearly its whole length, and terminating at a fort on the farm of John Brown. This was done by digging a ditch of a sufficient depth for the men in front, in case of an attack, to entrench themselves from the fire of the enemy. The earth that was excavated was thrown in such a position as to afford a similar entrenchment for those in the rear. My first recollection of this breastwork was when about five years of age. At that time, I suppose, the ditch was about three feet deep, though after a lapse of twenty-three years, it had been considerably filled up; and the embankment formed by the excavation, about the same height. A considerable portion of it is still (1850) remaining in a tolerable good state of preservation. Other similar ones, of shorter lengths, were erected in other places, to be used in cases of emergency.

On the rear line of encampment, a range of forts was erected, in a line nearly parallel with the Front Line, commencing on the land of David Stephens, and were called David Stephens' Forts and John Brown's Forts, on account of their being erected on the land of these individuals. I do not know of any forts or redoubts being erected on the Valley Forge estate, neither have I ever seen the remains of any upon any part of it, from which I conclude that there were none on that property. In many places, and particularly between the forts, picket guards were placed to obstruct the advance of cavalry in case of an attack. These were formed of rails with one end sharply pointed, the other placed firmly in the ground, the pointed end elevated at an angle of about fifteen degrees, and placed so closely together that a horseman could not pass between them. Many of the rails used for this purpose were left on the premises, and I have in my time seen many of them.

The distance from Valley Forge to the Front Line Hill, in a direct line, is about a mile and a half, which was the greatest width of the encampment. It was much narrower at its northeast and south-west terminations, the river Schuylkill and Valley Creek governing its breadth at these places.

As I shall have occasion to speak of the Rear Line Hill, as well as the Front Line Hill, I may here mention, that a hill forming the western boundary of the river Schuylkill and running nearly parallel with the Front Line, and leaving the course of the river near Headquarters, and continuing in the same direction up the Valley Creek to the county line, above where the old forge stood that was burned by the British, constituted the Rear Line Hill, and is the hill mentioned in my second letter.

It was on the ground occupying the space between these two lines, that the temporary huts, for the soldiers and some of the officers to winter in, were erected; the greater number of them on the farms of Mordecai Moore and David Stephens. The timber was cut down, and the huts or cabins put up in a short time after their arrival, for while a part of the soldiers were engaged in constructing fortifications and breastworks, others were cutting down timber and rearing their rude and miserable huts to shelter them from the severe winter that was approaching, and which was rendered still more so by their destitute and forlorn situation, as described; yet such was the energy with which they engaged in the undertaking, and the alacrity with which they, under every disadvantage, carried it on,, that I have understood that in the course of four days after their arrival the most of the work was completed.

I never saw any of the huts; they were all demolished before my time (1795); but the foundations of most of them were still visible. When I first remember visiting the ground, and from having so often seen them, I can form a just estimate of their size, and from the description given of them by my father. I trust that the information I shall give concerning them, will be generally correct. The greater number of the huts, judging from the foundations as they presented themselves, in my early days, varied in size from ten to sixteen feet square, occasionally the foundation of a much larger one presented itself among them. I always understood that a mess of seven men among the soldiers occupied one hut, and many of the inferior officers had single huts for their accommodation. The sites of many of the officers' huts and the names of their occupants were pointed out to me by my father, when I was about eight years of age. Directly on the rear of the breastwork on the Front Line Hill, and about twenty yards distant from it, a line of huts was constructed, commencing on the land of Mordecai Moore, and extending towards its southwestern termination. Traces of many of them are still visible, and they appear to have been erected in a nearly uniform line with spaces or passages between them like streets or roads. This regularity in their construction is most apparent on the front and rear lines. Towards the center less order appears to have been observed, as the remains or foundations of the huts clearly indicate. The principal part of the huts on the rear line and in the center were erected on the land of David Stephens, though a number of them were on the Valley Forge estate, and some few in the centre and on both lines were on the land of other persons. A small number were erected on both sides of the lines of encampment, but all traces of them have long since been obliterated, and their foundations ploughed up. I have a faint recollection of having seen the sites of some of them. These huts were constructed in a very rough and ready manner, and without the aid of the master builders and architects of the present day, for they were hastily built of logs, rudely jointed together in the manner of cribs, and the spaces between them filled up with stone, mud and clay, and whatever other materials the exegency of the case afforded, and covered with earth excavated from the cellars. They had no windows, and an opening was left in one end for a door. It was in this manner the temporary accommodations for the soldiers and some of the officers were hastily formed to shelter them, though very poorly, from the inclemency of the approaching winter. They had no attic or basement stories, they were barely high enough to admit a man to stand upright. Some of them had chimneys and places for fires, though the most of them had not this convenience, and their fires were generally built upon the ground on the outside of their cabins, and here they performed their cooking operations in a very simple and primitive way.

I have occasionally, in my rambles over the ground in my youthful days, in search of cows, which were turned upon it to pasture (for then the greater part of it either lay a common or was an unenclosed forest) found among the foundations of the huts, the remains of logs that had been used in their construction, and about thirty-nine years ago I found in one of them the remains of a chimney, in a tolerable state of preservation, and which I also saw some years afterwards, and a short time previous to my removing to this county, but not having traversed the grounds for the last twenty years, I cannot say whether or not it is still remaining. Upon mentioning these circumstances to my father, he informed me that these were the quarters of some of the general officers, who on account of the thinly settled state of the country could not obtain them at the dwellings of the inhabitants in the vicinity of the encampment.

The foregoing description may serve to give my readers a faint, but at best a very faint and imperfect idea, of the manner and kind of dwellings with which the soldiers were provided during that memorable campaign, and we may figure to our imaginations, from the destitute condition, and the want of the very necessaries of life under which they were laboring when they entered them, how much they suffered during their abode at the place. I shall now conclude this epistle, by observing that in my next I shall give some account of the general officers, and the place of their different quarters, and some other matters that I have heard related of that period, and probably some accounts of the outposts of the army that were placed as an advanced guard.

Valley Forge, Pa. Washington's Headquarters

Reception Room

Washington's Bedroom

The Office

First Floor Hall

INTERIORS OF WASHINGTON'S HEADQUARTERS

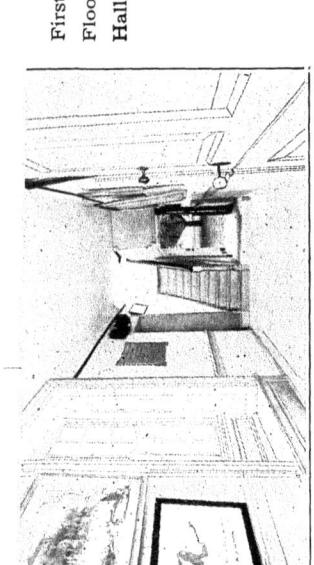

Kitchen Fireplace

LETTER XI

QUARTERS OF THE GENERAL OFFICERS

AVING in my last given a description of the huts that were hastily erected for a temporary shelter for the soldiers during the winter, I may now observe that, when finished, they collected leaves, dead grass, straw, hay, and other materials into their huts to lie upon; and each one having a blanket and knapsack, and seven of them occupying one hut, used their knapsacks for pillows, and their blankets for bed clothes to cover themselves; but they found food and clothing not so easily obtained; and for want of the latter they often suffered. In a former letter I mentioned that the quarters of the general officers had been designated by some of the subordinate ones, who preceded the main body of the army on the morning of their arrival; they were at the following places:

The headquarters of General Washington was at the house of a minister of the Society of Friends, named Isaac Potts, at the chief mansion at Valley Forge, at that time the largest house in that vicinity and best calculated for headquarters. At the house of David Stephens, it being the next below on the Schuylkill, General Varnum was quartered. Proceeding on to the next one, then occupied by Zachary Davis and belonging to David Stephens, General Huntingdon was quartered. At the next one on the river, then owned by William Smith, First Provost of the University of Pennsylvania, and occupied at the time by a man named Henry Force, the provost guard was stationed; and the officers having charge of it were quartered at the house. The next one on the river was then occupied by a man named Michael Shur; he used to boast of having had the command of the Second Regiment quartered at his house, but who the commander was, or to what brigade he belonged, fame has not informed us. I am not certain that any officers were qaurtered at any of the houses any lower down the river.

I shall now leave the course of it, and proceed to the house of John Moore, at the northeast extremity of the encampment. General Muhlenberg was quartered at the house of Mordecai Moore, which was the next one above in the Great Valley. General Morgan, when not engaged with his rangers on the outposts, was quartered, and also the Commissary General of the army, at the house of my grandfather, Abijah Stephens, it being the next adjoining farm and the place of my nativity. On the southeastern boundary, General Wheedon was quartered for a short time. General Mifflin had his headquarters at William Godfrey's; General Greene, at Isaac Walker's; Gen. Sullivan, at Thomas Waters'; Gen. Poor, at Benjamin Jones'; Gen. Potter, at Jacob Walter's; and Gen. Wayne, at the house of Joseph Walker—these constituting all the farms and houses at that time lying in the Valley in Chester county, on the southeastern and south sides of the encampment, except one at that time belonging to a German, named John Beaver, at whose house I have always understood that no officers were quartered.

On the southwestern extremity, I have always understood the following officers were quartered: Gen. Knox, at the house of John Havard; and Gen. Maxwell, at the house of John Brown; and on the west side of the Valley Creek, at Valley Forge, Gen. McIntosh was quartered at the house of a respectable colored person, named Joseph Mann.

I have now in my account travelled around the encampment ground and come back to headqaurters. I may just observe at this place, that at the time just alluded to, there were no dwelling houses in the limits of the ground, occupied by the main body of the army. Lafayette did not arrive here until some time after the army had encamped at the place. He came in company with DeKalb, Pulaski, Steuben, Kosciusko, Duloyson, and other distinguished foreigners, who joined our army, of some of whom and their quarters some notice will be taken in some of my future letters.

In addition to these, whose quarters have been mentioned, there were several officers of rank, but where they had quarters I cannot say with certainty, but conclude the most of them lived during the time in huts; and I well remember my father showing me the foundations of large huts and telling me they were occupied by officers during the time of the encampment; and on one occasion he pointed out the one that had been occupied by Gen. Lee. This was on the Valley Forge estate, on the north side of the Rear Line Hill. Among those that have not been noticed were Generals Conway, Smallwood, Armstrong, Furman, MacDougal, and many others not now recollected, the most of whom lived in the camp at the time.

I have heard it mentioned by persons living at the time that some officers were quartered at the houses of Samuel Jones and Samuel Richards, in the Great Valley, immediately above Joseph Walker's; but not having availed myself of proper information on the subject, I cannot say who they were. I should not suppose that any officers were quartered higher up the Valley than the latter place, as that was beyond the farthest extent of the picket guards in a southerly direction. I am further confirmed in this opinion from a circumstance mentioned to me by John Davis, one of the Associate Judges of the county of Chester, and who was at the time of the encampment at the Valley Forge, a captain in the regular army, and whose residence was on the Valley Creek, not more than four miles from the Valley Forge, where he was stationed. He informed me a short time previous to his being deprived of the use of speech by paralysis, that during the whole period the army was there, he was so constantly engaged that he was at home but twice during the time. While engaged in the service, he kept a journal of many of the occurrences of the camp, a part of which was published in 1823 in the *Village Record,* a paper published at West Chester at that time, by Hon. Charles Miner, and continued in weekly numbers for several months; and I regret that I cannot now refer to it, not having preserved the numbers, as it contained much interesting information on the subject.

DISPOSITION OF THE ARMY

Having now got the troops in their huts, and the general officers mostly in their quarters, it may now be the proper place to mention the disposition of the army, and the positions assigned them. After the fall of Gen. Nash, who commanded the troops constituting Washington's body or life guard, many of whom were slain at the battle of Germantown, the survivors of them were placed under the command of Gen. McIntosh, and as body guard to the commander-in-chief, were stationed on a hill a little east of Headquarters. On the hill of the Rear Line, and on both sides of the Gulf road, and extending in a southeasterly direction, were stationed the brigades of Generals Conway, Maxwell, Huntingdon and Varnum, the latter being stationed on a hill near his quarters, where a redoubt was erected in order to command a view of the opposite side of the river. The site of the redoubt, which is now so nearly destroyed as to leave but few traces of its existence remaining, was placed on an elevated point of land, from which an extensive view of both sides of the river could be secured, and so near the stream as to employ the artillery to check an attempt of the enemy to cross over near the place; but their use for the purpose was never required.

The main body of the army under the command of Generals Muhlenberg, Wheedon, Mifflin, Poor, Potter and Wayne, were stationed along the Front Line Hill; and troops under the command of the several officers last named, were so arranged as to be nearest their respective quarters. The division of Sullivan was stationed on the Schuylkill between Headquarters and the Fatland ford, about half a mile lower down the river; some further notice of them will be given in a future number. The troops commanded by Knox and Smallwood, and afterwards by Lafayette, were stationed on the southeastern extremity of the encampment.

The artillery, under command of Col. Proctor, were stationed on the south side of the Gulf road, between that and the Baptist road in the county of Montgomery, a little north of the Chester county line—the place ever since retaining the name of the park. In case of attack from the enemy the direction of the artillery was to be given to Gen. Duportale, chief of the engineers. The foregoing is nearly as correct an account as I can give from memory, as the circumstances have been related to me, by many persons who were conversant with these things and the passing events of the day; but my informants are now no more in this state of existence.

The outposts mentioned in my last were placed to watch the movements of the enemy, act as an advanced guard, surprise foraging parties of the enemy, and intercept any communications between the disaffected people of that day with the British; and also to prevent trading with them, as there were even some, who, though not adhering to the cause of royalty, yet for the sake of a hard currency, which could always be obtained of the enemy, in preference to the depreciating paper money of that day, ventured at all hazards to trade with them. A line of these outposts commenced at the river Schuylkill opposite the place where the town of Conshohocken now stands; then known by the name of Matson's Ford, extending in a southwesterly direction several miles; that portion of country, lying between the main body at Valley Forge and the outposts, being on the prescribed lines of the army. The command of these was given to Gen. Lord Sterling, who was encamped near the Schuylkill on the Gulf Hills, and from this circumstance the place was known as Rebel Hill, a name it still retains. The General while here was quartered at the house of John Reese; and among other officers attached to his brigade, and with him at his quarters, was James Monroe, since President of the United States, and one of the most popular men that has ever filled the executive chair. This house is now standing, having undergone but little if any alteration since that time. It is now occupied by a sister of my mother, now in the eighty-second year of her age, and the last survivor of that generation, and nearly the last one of the Revolution, who was a resident of the neighborhood of Valley Forge, at the time of the encampment, who was of an age sufficient to remember the passing events of that day. I shall have occasion to speak of her more fully hereafter.

As mentioned in the forepart of this letter, the rangers of Gen. Morgan were placed on the outposts, his place of rendezvous being on the farm on which Morgan's on the Columbia Railroad is now located; and at the house of Mordecai Morgan, at the original mansion, he had his headquarters when in the neighborhood. I have understood that the General was distantly related to this family, but on this point I cannot speak correctly; it was from the latter family that the name of Morgan's Corner was called. Here he was said to be particularly useful in preventing many from trading with the British, by supplying them with provisions and otherwise holding communication with them. While thus engaged, I never heard of any further violent measures being used by him upon any thus surprised and captured, than to secure their produce and then let them return home. He captured some persons from York county, who, with teams were engaged in removing to Philadelphia the furniture of a person mentioned in a former letter, who was taken out of prison by his wife; they let the people go, but secured the goods. Other similar detachments were placed at different stations for similar purposes and a skirmish took place at the house of a person named John Scott in Easttown township, Chester county, between one of these and a foraging party of the enemy, in which one person was killed and several wounded. Major William Brooke of Radnor township, Delaware county, was the officer who commanded on the occasion. One of the persons wounded at the time was a person named Griffith Reese, a brother to George Reese, sheriff of the city and county of Philadelphia about eighteen years ago. I may also add in this place that the Major Brooke just mentioned is the same whom some of my readers may remember, who after living to an advanced age and enjoyed a respectable standing in the community, in the year 1829 was killed by a blow inflicted by his own son, while laboring under a partial aberration of mind.

I shall now close this subject as relates to the general arrangement and disposition of the army; and in my next will relate some incidents that occurred during the time; and endeavor, as far as in my power, to give a description of the hardships and trials that were suffered by them during that severe season.

LETTER XII

INCIDENTS OF THE CAMP

HE ARMY was now partially sheltered from the inclemency of the wind and weather, but still the prospect was far from being a bright one, for "shadows, clouds and darkness" rested upon it. For many weeks after, they suffered for want of food, blankets, and clothes, particularly shoes. Provisions of all kinds were nearly exhausted, their blankets nearly worn out, their clothes, not only tattered and torn, but from long use worn threadbare and scarcely holding together, and the prospect of a further supply, from the reduced state of the country, very precarious. But their greatest suffering was for want of shoes. I have often heard it related by many persons living in the neighborhood that they had seen the snow and ground over which the soldiers had to pass in performing the duties of the camp, marked with the blood that flowed from their feet, and while they beheld these things, and looked upon the objects of suffering, shivering with cold, and suffering from hunger, which it was not in their power fully to relieve, they have admired the magnanimity and firmness with which they bore all their trials. In addition to those just narrated, there were many other hardships they had to undergo; that cruel scourge, the small-pox, was introduced into the camp, threatening to destroy all who had not been innoculated. Owing to neglect or inability on the part of Congress, the commissary department became so exhausted that there was, at one time, not a day's provisions of any kind on hand, and absolute famine threatened them. Some of the troops had been a week, and others three or four days, without a mouthful of animal food of any kind. Yet, under all these discouragements, they patiently endured their sufferings for several weeks without a murmur. To enumerate all their sufferings that I have heard related, would swell these narrations to an unreasonable length. I shall, therefore, omit many things which, if inserted, would be tautologous.

I shall now refer to a disposition which many among them began to manifest, to leave the army and return to their homes. This disposition had been created and fostered by some leading demagogues, circulating anonymous letters among them, censuring Congress, on account of not supplying them with the necessaries they required, and secretly encouraging them to revolt and forsake the cause they had espoused. A favorable time to effect

THE HISTORY OF VALLEY FORGE

their object had been embraced, when the affairs of Congress were at their lowest ebb, and the army in the distressed situation just described, and the country surrounding the encampment, and upon the bounty of which some of them had for some time been supported, had become nearly destitute of provisions and other necessaries. Their love for their commander-in-chief and other officers, and their devotion to their country's freedom, had thus far kept them united, and it was now only the influence of Washington that prevented an open revolt. He reasoned pathetically with them on the impropriety of leaving the army, and lost no time in representing their sufferings to Congress. They then agreed to continue with him without repining. At this particular juncture of time, such was the scarcity of the means of transporting the supplies for the use of the army, that the soldiers and even some of the officers, like beasts of burden, performed with cheerfulness, the duties of providing and carrying wood, provisions and other necessaries for the use of their suffering companions, for there were at this time near three thousand persons so destitute of clothing as to be unfit for duty; fires had to be kept up during the night to prevent them from perishing with cold, and many others from sickness and wounds, were crowded into hospitals and private houses, claiming that attention necessary on such occasions, but which on account of the destitute condition of the government they could not fully receive.

Upon application being made to Congress, and a true representation of the condition of the troops accompanying it, that body appointed a committee to visit them, who, after the performance of their duty and making report, which was done as expeditiously as possible, such relief and assistance was given as the slender means in their power afforded. But the winter, owing to their destitute condition, was one of uncommon severity, and many ended their days in the service at this place, especially those stationed on the north side of the Rear Line Hill, who were generally from the southern colonies, and not accustomed to the climate, and being in a more exposed situation, many of them died in consequence, and their mortal remains were laid there without a stone to mark the spot where their "mouldering ashes sleep," but not "low in the ground," for they were often buried so near the surface as to be disinterred by hungry swine, and in places where the soil has been washed off, the decaying bones have been presented to view, some of which I have seen within the last thirty years (between 1820 and 1850).

In the midst of these trying scenes, an attempt was made to remove Washington from the chief command, and place Gen. Gates, then exulting in his triumph in the capture of Burgoyne, in his stead. Whether the latter was concerned in the affair I have not distinctly understood. Generals Lee and Conway, neither of them native Americans, and some other officers, together with some members of Congress, were believed to be at the head of the movement. Measures were used to bring Lafayette to unite in the scheme, but these, together with the whole project, proved an entire failure, and Washington, to the joy of the army at this place, and the majority of the people of the nation, continued in command. Soon after this his wife came from Mt. Vernon to spend the residue of the campaign with him at Headquarters.

It may be in place here to relate what I have often heard said of Washington, by many persons of the place, that during this, and all other gloomy periods of the Revolution, his confidence in the final triumph of freedom and the cause of liberty, and the final success of the army under his command, never forsook him. While he felt for the trials of those under his command, and suffered with them, and his benevolent heart bled for their sufferings, and as far as in his power, endeavored to mitigate them, yet in his duty to his country, that had entrusted so great a task to him to perform he stood firm and unmoved, comparable to a rock firmly planted on the shore of a tempestuous ocean, against which the wind and waves and adverse storms, may beat with all their combined fury, but are unable to remove, or even shake it from its centre. To this, may in a great measure, be attributed his peculiar faculty of winning and securing the affections of the army at that critical time, and of their calmly listening to his parental advice, when on the brink of a revolt as noticed above. And it was from this source, and the unshaken confidence in the goodness of his cause, that on the occasion they reliquished their intentions, and quietly and cheerfully again resumed the severe hardships and self-denying duties of the camp. In this confidence he stood not alone; there was a host of others, equally sanguine, and who endured, with equal firmness, many severe trials and disappointments, and firmly adhered and remained devoted to the cause they had espoused, during that memorable winter; time would fail to tell of all. I shall merely mention the names of Greene, Sullivan, Wayne, Mifflin, DeKalb and Lafayette, omitting a number of others equally patriotic and firm in their adherence to the cause of freedom. There is one, however inconsistent his conduct may appear to many, as a professed minister of Christian religion, and incompatible with the gospel of truth, yet his patriotism and devotion to the cause, and his firmness in adhering to it, during the gloomy period of the Revolution, may claim a few passing remarks. I mean the Rev. David Jones, chaplain to General Wayne's brigade, and for many years pastor of the Baptist congregation in the Great Valley. He early manifested a deadly hatred and hostility to the measures of the British government, and soon after the commencement of the Revolution, pub-

The History of Valley Forge

lished a work in vindication of defensive war. I have understood that it was his practice to preach at different stations during the time, and to encourage the officers and soldiers in his discourses, to persevere in contending against their enemies, frequently on these occasions using for his texts the fourteeth and nineteenth verses of the fourth chapter of the book of Nehemiah.

During the encampment at Valley Forge, I have heard it said that Washington used often to retire to solitary places, and on one of these occasions, he was discovered by Isaac Potts engaged in vocal prayer. This circumstance is noticed by Weems in his life of Washington, and some comments made upon it by the author, of this circumstance concerning Isaac Potts, of the consistency of the sword and the Gospel. How far the account of this convincement is correct I am not prepared to say, as it is the only account I have ever seen or heard of it. But I have heard the circumstance related, and the spot was pointed out to me several years before I saw the account published. And while I am not prepared to adopt the conclusion that Mr. Potts was thus convinced of the consistency of the sword and the Gospel, yet through the remainder of his life he was always a warm friend of Washington, and always spoke of him in terms of the highest respect. I was once told by a near relative of his, that previous to the time alluded to, he was unsettled in his adherence to the American cause, but his intimate acquaintance with Washington removed his objections, and in his latter days he was a firm republican in principle and practice.

As I shall not have much more to say of the general sufferings of the camp, but shall in my future communications confine myself to other matters of a more special nature that occurred during the time, I will just add before closing, that among those who were stationed here, enduring the sufferings and privations of that day, were many of the wealthy and respectable from all parts of the Union, and from the South there were some individuals, who have since filled important offices in the government, among whom may be mentioned the Butlers, Claibornes, Blounts, Lewises, Macons, Merrewethers, and many others from various parts of the Union, whose names are not recollected. In some of my future communications, I shall have further reference to the subject.

LETTER XIII

MORE ABOUT WHEEDON

N ONE of my former letters some notice was given of General Wheedon, and also of my intention of giving some further information concerning him. It has been observed that he remained at his quarters but a short time, but short as it was, it was long enough for the soldiers under his command to commit depredations to so great an extent, that it required years to overcome the effects, and to restore the waste places produced in consequence of their rapacity. Almost every tree on the place was cut down or destroyed; all the fences were either used for fuel, or carried off the premises, to be employed in constructing huts, or forming picket guards. Their hay, grain, straw, fodder and vegetables, were all taken, as the General said, for the use of the army; but the real object was believed to be for the sole purpose of serving his own private interests. He exercised no restraint over the soldiers in this particular, the consequence was that all their movable property, not secured or removed beyond their reach, was taken by the soldiers with impunity, and the family were left nearly destitute of even the common domestic utensils, such as buckets, pots, kettles, pans, plates, knives and forks, and such things as were indispensably necessary. During the time of his quarters there, these depredations were committed, and I have often heard it related by many of the family that the only thing not previously secured, that escaped their rapacity, was a grindstone, which the General had ordered not to be removed on account of the daily use they made of it to grind their knives and other edge tools. I have heretofore hinted at his severity to his soldiers; he always kept a strong guard at the house, and during the most inclement nights, exposed to all kinds of weather, the poor soldiers thus employed, walked to and fro through the yard, poorly fed and still more poorly clad. Often in the dead hours of the night, would some of the members of the family arise from their beds, and from the window of the second story of the house, which was the only part the family occupied, throw to the poor famished guards pieces of meat, crusts of bread, and any kind of provisions they had on hand, which, while shuddering with cold, they would seize with avidity, and devour with the greediness of a ravenous animal.

His own aggrandizement and the acquisition of wealth seems

to have been his leading motive in entering the service, and the accomplishment of these objects his governing principle. He had a number of private baggage wagons, conducted by his own slaves, and used for the purpose of conveying supplies for the use of the army, often at extravagant prices, which were extorted from the government on account of its necessitous situation, and at all times embracing every opportunity in his power to speculate on the public treasury, receiving his pay in continental money. But nearly enough has been said of him, unless it were better, and I shall soon take leave of him, by just mentioning that having in various ways accumulated a large amount of Continental money, and fearing it would die on his hands, he sold his teams, collected his slaves, resigned his commission, and returned to his home, to invest his money in real estate, and this is the last account I ever heard of him.

DEKALB SUCCEEDS WHEEDON

Upon the resignation of Wheedon, the command of the Virginia line was given to Baron DeKalb, a German nobleman, whose character, life, services and death at Camden, in South Carolina, are too well known to need a description here. He also succeeded to the quarters of Wheedon, at my grandfather's, and soon a different state of things were produced, and, while less servile homage was paid to his person by the soldiers, their affections were more firmly secured by his kind and affectionate treatment to them, at the same time his authority was more firmly established, and his orders obeyed, and more restraint placed over the soldiers; order and regularity were restored, and the situation of the family much more pleasant than it had been previous to his arrival. The family having been supplied with things necessary for domestic purposes, by some of their relatives and friends, who lived beyond the scenes of devastation, the property was, through his authority, protected from much further depredation. His urbanity rendered him an agreeable companion, and laid the foundation of a lasting friendship between them. Much more might be related concerning the Baron, during his residence at the house, for I call it his residence, as he was there more than four months, and was always considered as one of the family; and from the day of his arrival until he left the place, he was always viewed more as an old friend and acquaintance than a perfect stranger from a foreign land. After leaving the place, whenever opportunity offered, a correspondence was kept up between him and my grandfather, and his last letter was written a few days previous to the battle of Camden, where he fell, and not received until some weeks after his death. This letter I regret has been lost. Another that was written a few weeks previous is still in possession of the family, and was published in this and some other papers of this county about two years since.

I have often heard his person and habits described by my mother; he was tall of stature, and very erect for a person of his years, being more than sixty years of age, having been forty years in the Prussian service. He had a very open intelligent countenance, dark blue eyes, very expressive, a good set of teeth, well formed head, his hair grey, and his complexion, from long exposure, rather swarthy; in his habits, temperate and abstemious; his conversation, bland and interesting, and manners polite and agreeable, given to sociability—a man of liberal education, speaking the English language well for a foreigner. I have heard her say he would sit for hours together with the family on long winter evenings, in relating incidents and many interesting accounts that had taken place under his immediate notice in Europe, one of which was a very lively account of a journey to his native place, a little time before his embarking for this country, to visit his aged parents, whom he had not seen for more than twenty years. The distance was about two hundred miles. His father and mother were then about eighty-seven years of age, both of them enjoying good health and unimpaired faculties, and capable of performing bodily labor. They were not in affluent circumstances, and the Baron had risen to preferment, not through the influence of wealth or claims to nobility, but through his own merit, having in early youth been accustomed to labor. He used to relate that when he arrived at his father's house, he found his aged mother busily engaged at her spinning, enjoying that satisfaction that can be felt only by those who can look in the evening of their day, on the reward of a well-spent life. Upon inquiry for his father, he was informed that he was at work in a wood a short distance from the house; and shortly after he went out to seek him, and met him returning home in company with a grandson, each laden with billets of wood for fuel. The meeting was a joyful one to all parties. When relating these circumstances, he used to mention it as one of the happiest days of his life, recalling to his mind the fond recollections of early days and the joyous scenes of his youth, which all the honors that had been conferred upon him had not been able to obliterate. His visiting his aged parents and spending some time with them in retirement, afforded him a satisfaction far superior to the din of battle, the noise of folly, the adulation of flattery, the tinsel of honor, or the baubles of royalty. The circumstances of this journey were themes of conversation he used to love to dwell upon, and which he hoped again to witness, when his mission in this country should be accomplished. But this hope was never realized. At the battle of Camden, in South Carolina, he fell pierced with wounds, and soon breathed his last, far from his native home, and all his tender connections in life. I have an idea that at the time he was here, he was a widower, and had left a family of children in Prussia; but whether or not this is correct, I am not certain. If it were so, it may be one cause of his particular fondness for the children of the family, some of whom at that time were small. He used to treat them with great kindness, and in hours of relaxation would enjoy himself with their childish sports, always trying to please them and gain their affections.

It may now be in place to mention a small matter related to me a few weeks since, by the only surviving one of the family living at that period—the venerable Elizabeth Reese, now living at the quarters of Lord Sterling, near the Gulf Hills, in the eighty-second year of her age. At the time he was at her father's house, she was in the ninth year of her age, and was always his particular favorite. When about to leave the place, upon taking an affectionate leave of the family, when bidding her an affectionate and final farewell, he took from his breast a ribbon, to which was fastened a star, which he always wore as a badge of his nobility, and presented it to her, telling her to keep it in remembrance of him. She kept it for a short time, when a little girl from a distance came to see her, and wanting it, she, to use her own words, "foolishly gave it away," and it was never recovered. When mentioning the circumstance, she expressed her regret at having parted with it, not that it was of any great value, but that now in her old age of having it to look upon, and of having kept it in accordance with his request.

During his residence at the place he always enjoyed himself agreeably, partook at the same table with the family, frequently furnishing them from his private stores, with many things that the situation of the family required, but could not be easily obtained on account of foreign trade being suspended, and but few if any manufactories being put in operation, and where any efforts were made to establish them, they were destroyed by the enemy, it being their policy to make the colonies as dependent as possible upon foreign nations, for all the necessaries of life. And such was the confidence reposed in the Baron, that I have often heard it related, that in a few instances when the heads of the family had to leave home for a few days, the family and domestic affairs were left in his charge, and were cheerfully undertaken by him, and his duties were faithfully attended to and discharged. On occasions exercising a parental care over the family, and a more rigid discipline over the soldiers and officers under his command. I might add much more concerning him if it were necessary; enough has been said to give an idea of his general character, and the friendship that existed between him and the family.

LETTER XIV

OTHER DISTINGUISHED FOREIGNERS

MONG the foreigners that arrived at Valley Forge in company with Baron DeKalb, one of the most noted was LaFayette, who, having been wounded at the battle of Brandywine, did not come with the main body of the army, but remained in order to recover from his wound, and if I mistake not, somewhere in the neighborhood of the battle ground. He took up his quarters at the house of Samuel Havard, about two miles south of Headquarters, on the Valley Creek, and remained there during the residue of the campaign. He used frequently to visit DeKalb at his quarters, which introduced the Marquis to an acquaintance with my grandfather's family. Of the other distinguished ones were Pulaski and Kosciusko, celebrated Polish officers; the first was slain at the battle of Savannah, and the second some years after the war returned to his native country, and was commander-in-chief of the armies of Poland at the time of their final overthrow, at the battle of the Bridge of Prague, by the combined armies of Russia, Austria and Prussia, and with the fall of whom perished the liberties of Poland, as Campbell the poet, in his vivid description of it, has observed,

"Hope for a season bade the world farewell,
And freedom shrieked as Kosciusko fell."

Dupertale and Duponceau, French officers of whom I may hereafter take some notice, Baron Steuben and Dubryson, Prussian officers, and many others that I have heard of, some of whose names I have heard, and others I have not heard, or if I heard, cannot now recollect; neither is it very material, as the most of them were not so conspicuous as those above noticed. I shall therefore pass them by at this time.

DUBRYSON'S CAVE

Dubryson, who was the particular friend of DeKalb during the time he was there, dwelt in a cave on the premises and near the house of my grandfather, the foundation of which remained till 1811, being for many years used as a place to break flax in. That year the present mansion house on the farm was erected and the foundation of the cave filled up, and a part of the ground now forming the front yard covers the site of Dubryson's cave. Pulaski I have understood (since writing a former letter) after his arrival had his quarters in the house of John Beaver, with the widow and family; John Beaver died a short time previous to the arrival of the army. The others might have had their quarters in huts in the encampment, as I never heard of any of them having them at any of the houses in the neighborhood. They all used to visit Baron DeKalb at his quarters, as I have been informed by different members of the family. When I was between eight and nine years of age, having had frequent occasion to pass through the encampment ground with my father, and in one of these he pointed out to me the foundations of a large hut, and told me it had been occupied as the quarters of Baron Steuben. This was on the farm of Maurice Stephens, now belonging to William Henry, one of the present representatives in the General Assembly from the county of Montgomery, and on the same farm on which General Hutingdon was quartered. He at the same time facetiously observed that the place over which we were then passing was called Steuben's Kitchen, from an incident that occurred when he took possession of it, which he then related to me, nearly as follows:

STEUBEN'S KITCHEN

The Baron was a man of wealth and something of an epicure, had brought with him from Europe a man who was a professed cook, the Baron possibly expecting to live in the same style and fare as sumptuously as he had in his own country. If so he met with disappointment. When the cook went to prepare dinner, on inquiring for the kitchen and cooking utensils, was directed to a fire outside the hut, around which forks were driven in the ground, and from poles placed upon them were pieces of meat suspended by strings, hanging before the fire to roast; and was told that the place where the fire was burning was the kitchen, and the strings by which the pieces of meat were suspended, the cooking utensils. The cook replied that the services of a man of his abilities were not required in America, and he would return to Europe. He soon after quitted the service, and returned home to employ his talents there, not relishing Steuben's Kitchen. Numerous other anecdotes and reminiscences of that period that I have often heard related, many of them by persons who witnessed them, might be related were they deemed of sufficient importance to claim the attention of my readers; the most of them will therefore be omitted, together with many other incidents that occurred in the neighborhood of the encampment during the time of its continuance there, as the recital of them would be tedious, and requires more time than I can now give the subject.

SULLIVAN'S BRIDGE

In a former number, I mentioned the place where Sullivan's men were stationed, and promised to give some further information concerning it. As before noticed, they were placed on the river Schuylkill, between Headquarters and Fatland Ford. During the time of the encampment at the place, Sullivan and his hardy New England boys constructed a bridge over the river, in order to facilitate their passage across in case they should be compelled to make a hasty retreat from the place, and to afford them more ready means of obtaining necessaries from the opposite side. This was done in the spring of 1778, by building piers in the river and placing timbers upon them in a rough and ready manner. What method they took to erect these pillars in the channel I have never learned. They were placed much nearer together than our modern bridges, and the span formed of one piece of timber, extending from one pier to another. The foundations of these pillars are, for aught I know, still remaining; when the water was low they could be distinctly seen. I have often seen them previous to the river being made navigable by slack water navigation; since that time, the water being raised by a dam constructed about two miles lower down the river, they are covered several feet under water, and the only object to mark the spot where the bridge once stood, is a stone placed on the bank opposite the place with the inscription on it of "Sullivan's Bridge, 1778." But I have got in advance of my narrative, and I must now return to Sullivan and his men.

It has been several times noticed in former communications, that provisions were very scarce during that winter, to which we may also add that various means were resorted to in order to procure them; and it may be in place here to relate a circumstance that was related to me, of the means made use of by these sturdy New Englanders to procure food. The account was given me by Henry Pawling, Esq., father of the late Levi Pawling of Norristown, an eminent lawyer, for many years at the head of the Montgomery county bar, and a representative in the 17th Congress. Henry Pawling, who, at the time of the encampment, owned the property immediately opposite the place, and who resided all his life time on the same farm, informed me that he had often seen them during the winter, when the water was clear and not frozen over, wading in the water, braving the inclemency of the weather to hunt muscles for food, and when thus engaged they would jocosely observe that fresh water clams made good soup.

I have often heard a story related concerning the bridge, before removing to this county, and since my residence here, I met with an aged man, an officer in the Revolutionary Army, who was encamped there, and present at the time the conversation took place. I allude to General Samuel Smith, late of Buckingham township, deceased, who related the circumstance nearly as I had always heard it from others. After the work was finished, Sullivan invited General Washington and a number of other officers, with some people of the neighborhood, to come and see it and take a walk over it. A number of the officers and others complied with the request, among whom was David Stephens, who, residing near the place, was probably better acquainted with the freshets that occurred in the river, and particularly those upon the breaking up of the ice, than any of them present, was asked by Sullivan his opinion of the stability of the bridge, and how long he supposed it would stand, informed him that it might possibly stand till the next ice flood, but he was certain that upon the next breaking up of the ice, if accompanied by a heavy flood, it would be carried off. Sullivan, who was rather profane in his language, though in other respects an amiable and benevolent man, replied in language I shall not repeat, his assurance of the durability of his structure by positively declaring that all the ice floods that ever were or would be in the Schuylkill would not ever be able to destroy it. It stood during the ensuing summer, but at the breaking up of the ice at the close of the next winter, it was, with the exception of the piers, carried away; and thus ended Sullivan's Bridge. One great cause of its being so soon carried off, was owing to its not being sufficiently high to admit the water and ice to pass under it; and the materials of which the passage was composed were so slightly put together, that they were unable either to stand a heavy pressure or a sudden rise of the stream. If I should judge from the remains of the piers, I should say the bridge was much narrower than similar structures of the present day, probably not more than twelve feet in width; three pieces of timber extended from one pier to another across the stream, and upon these were laid pieces of timber for flooring, formed by splitting a log into two equal parts, the flat sides turned towards the water, and fastened to the sleepers by boring holes through them, and fastening them with wooden pins. I think I have heard it related that during the time of the encampment the river did not rise to so great a height as it generally did during the winter, that the ice and snow gradually melted and passed off, without doing much damage, which may have been the cause of Sullivan's confidence in the durability of his bridge, which subsequently proved futile.

I shall now draw the present communication to a close, by observing that in my next I shall have occasion to refer to some occurrences that took place during the time of the encampment, and also to have reference to the surrounding country after the close of the winter, and while the soldiers remained there in order to show, if possible, the dreary prospect that presented itself, and the discouragement under which the inhabitants labored.

LETTER XV

SUFFERINGS OF CIVILIANS

HE commencement of the year 1778 was to people residing in the vicinity of Valley Forge, and to the army encamped there, one of deep interest, the remembrance of which was never erased from the minds of those who passed through that trying season, and were of sufficient age to recollect them. Those who were residents of the neighborhood, and engaged in the active duties of life, felt the severe effects of having the army encamped in their borders, on account of the losses they sustained, on account of requisitions that were forcibly made upon them for necessaries for the army; while the soldiers suffered more than language can describe, from the combined effects of hunger, cold, sickness, want of clothing and almost everything essential to either comfort or convenience. The consequence was that of a general distraint being made upon all persons residing in the neighborhood of the fruits of their labor, and the products of their mills and farms, for the support of the great body of men encamped there—the number being about eleven thousand—all of whom had to be fed and otherwise provided with the necessaries of life. In effecting these objects the country soon became exhausted of provisions, the timberland in the immediate vicinity of the encampment was soon cleared off, the fences destroyed, the stock and poultry taken for the use of the army, and frequently by theft. It is an old adage that necessity knows no law; and the officers and soldiers at that time, and under the exigency of the occasion, seem to have been governed by it. The result was that many families, who, if not previously wealthy, were in good circumstances, and enjoying full and plenty of the real necessaries and comforts of life, were reduced to almost actual want.

SOLDIERS AS BEASTS OF BURDEN

Before the opening of spring, the fuel necessary for keeping the half clad warm was so far exhausted that a further supply had to be carried or brought from a distance; and such was the scarcity of the means of conveyance at the time, that it had to be brought to the camp by manual labor. Often have I heard people, who remembered the time, mention their having seen the soldiers, particularly those from the Eastern States, and some of the subordinate officers, yoke themselves together like oxen, and on temporary sleds formed for the occasion, haul fuel in this manner from a considerable distance, eight, ten, or more of them forming a team, and using grape vines to draw them by instead of ropes. And when the provisions and other necessaries in the immediate vicinity of the place became in like manner exhausted, requisitions had to be made from those living more remote from the scene; and foraging parties were accordingly sent to scour various portions of country, in order to secure sustenance for the famishing army; and when thus obtained, the conveyance of them to the place was often attended with great trouble and inconvenience, so that it is evident that much suffering and distress, both to the people and the army were the attendant consequence.

HOSPITALS

Yet, under all these trials they spent a period of near seven months, during which time, as before noticed, the small-pox was introduced into the camp, and many died from the effects of it; and hospitals and infirmaries had to be provided for those laboring under the disease. Previous to the encampment at the place, the sick and those that had been wounded at the battles of Brandywine, Germantown and the massacre of Paoli have been removed to Lancaster and Ephrata in Lancaster county, Reading in Berks county, the neighborhood of the Yellow Springs in Chester county, and other places, where hospitals had been provided for them. For the accommodation of those taken sick in the camp, the Friends' and Baptists' meeting houses in the Valley were taken possession of, and used for hospitals and infirmaries. For those laboring under contagious diseases, temporary ones were made a short distance beyond the lines of the camp, the location of one in particular I can point out; and many, both soldiers and officers, were placed in barns and private houses. Having thus passed through the winter, under all these disadvantages, spring as usual opened with all her beauty; but such was the state of the country, that no agricultural business could be carried on; the encampment still remained there; the crops of winter grain that had been sown the preceding fall, were destroyed; the fruitful fields laid waste; their stock or farming utensils lost or carried off; and nothing but the most dreary prospect presented itself, and the inhabitants and their families had to depend upon other sources for a supply of the common necessaries of life.

I may almost add, that in addition to that portion of the army who came here with the commander-in-chief, re-inforcements were arriving at different times during the campaign from the northern army, as their services after the capture of Burgoyne, were not so necessary in that section of country, they were sent to augment the forces at this place. This caused an additional demand for things necessary for their support, and increased the burden of the already suffering inhabitants of the place. The meeting house belonging to the Society of Friends in the Valley (the main part of the building still remaining) being occupied by the army for a hospital, they were prevented from holding their meetings at the place; but they assembled on their stated meeting days at the house of Isaac Walker, near the place, often having company of some of the officers, particularly Gen. Greene, who had been a member of the Society, and who, with others that attended, always conducted themselves in an orderly and becoming manner.

ABOUT SOME OF THE OFFICERS

The officers who were quartered in different places in the neighborhood, of whom no special notice has been taken, I have always heard them spoken of as men of agreeable manners and social dispositions, though some of them had their peculiarities and eccentricities, yet they all endeavored to render the situation of the families as comfortable as lay in their power, and to prevent as little damage as possible being done to their property, so that their company might be as easy and agreeable as the circumstances under which they were intruded upon, would permit. Of the commander-in-chief, nothing need be said, as his fame in public and private life needs no further eulogium; and abler pens have done justice to him, and his memory lives in the hearts of a grateful people. Of the others I shall notice only a few; among these are Greene, Wayne and Lafayette, of whom I have heard most notice taken.

Greene was very affable in his conversation, of agreeable manners, and handsome person, rather under the middle size, having the shrewdness peculiar to the people of New England; his health was delicate, but he preserved it by his temperate and regular habits.

Wayne, at that time, was about thirty-two years of age, healthy and active, of strong muscular powers, a Pennsylvania farmer by profession, rather above the middle size, with a fine ruddy countenance, and lively, expressive eyes. Though called Mad Anthony, on account of his daring courage when engaged in battle, his firmness of character and determined resolution, united with a hasty temper; yet in all his intercourse he was affable and agreeable, not only to the inhabitants of the neighborhood, but to the officers and men under his command, and remarkable for his amiable behavior and polite and accomplished manners in private

COMMANDER-IN-CHIEF

George Washington

MAJOR GENERALS

Dekalb	Mifflin
Greene	Steuben
Lafayette	Sterling
Lee	Sullivan

BRIGADIER GENERALS

Armstrong	Patterson
DuPortale	Poor
Glover	Scott
Huntingdon	Smallwood
Knox	Varnum
Learned	Wayne
McIntosh	Weedon
Maxwell	Woodford
Muhlenberg	

The Generals of the Continental Army at Valley Forge as given on the National Arch.

Naked and starving as they are
we cannot enough admire
the incomparable patience and fidelity
of the soldiery
—Washington at Valley Forge, Feb. 16, 1778.

And here
in this place
of sacrifice
in this valley of humiliation
in this valley of the shadow
of that death out of which
the life of America rose
regenerate and free
let us believe
with an abiding faith
that to them
union will seem as dear
and liberty as sweet
and progress as glorious
as they were to our fathers
and are to you and me
and that the institutions
which have made us happy
preserved by the
virtue of our children
shall bless
the remotest generation
of the time to come
—Henry Armitt Brown.

The Nation, on her Arch, at Valley Forge, through
two of her Sons.

life. He was a man of good education, an excellent mathematician, and for several years previous to the war, while residing on his paternal estate, near Paoli, following the occupation of a farmer, and if I mistake not of a tanner. He had also been much engaged as a practical surveyor, through different sections of the country about Valley Forge, which gave him a thorough knowledge of the location and people of the neighborhood, to many of whom he was related, his place of residence being in Easttown township, Chester county, about six miles from the encampment. I may probably give some further notice concerning it in a future number.

Lafayette at this time was young, not more than twenty-one years of age. He was married and had left his wife in France. I have heard it said by those who have had an opportunity of being acquainted with him, that he was a very handsome person, with a fine, open and intelligent countenance, his hair red, his movements light and active, though not fully recovered from the wound he received at the battle of Brandywine, and possessing all the open frankness, vivacity and colloquial powers so peculiar of the people of France. I may in some future numbers have occasion to have some further reference to him.

Lee and Conway, both foreigners, the one a native of England, the other of Ireland, were remarkable for their high and domineering spirits, and McIntosh for many singular peculiarities and credulity. I might add much more concerning Sullivan, Mifflin, Muhlenberg, Potter and many others, whose amiable dispositions and gentlemanly conduct, rendered them agreeable companions in the different families where they were quartered; and when they left the place, the most of them left a favorable impression and an esteem for them in after life. To dwell longer on the subject would be a mere repetition; I shall now pass from it to other matters.

In collecting these accounts, and endeavoring to recall to recollection what I have heard in days that are past and gone forever, I find many things occur to recall to remembrance facts that I have heard related of that period, by many persons who were witnesses to the passing events of the time, which, to use an oft quoted phrase, "tried men's souls," all of whom with one exception are now no longer in this state of existence, the most of which I would gladly insert, but they crowd upon my mind to so great an extent, that I must omit the most of them, some of which had better be buried in utter oblivion. I have now given an account of many of the principal events that transpired in connection with the encampment—of the distressed situation of the army upon their arrival at the place, the complicated sufferings and hardships they underwent during the time they continued there, of the combination to remove Washington from the command of the army, and many other matters that occurred previous to and about the time of their arrival, and during their continuance there. I now leave to the imagination of my readers to supply the deficiency, if any. And as there are yet some occurrences of the time that may justly claim further notice, I shall now draw this communication to a conclusion, and in my next I shall give an account of some few transactions that occurred at the place, as I have no recollection of ever seeing them published, that may possibly be of some interest to persons of the present day, especially such as feel an interest in obtaining information concerning that interesting time that our ancestors passed through, to purchase the freedom and liberty we now enjoy.

LETTER XVI

ALARMS AND LOSSES

S MENTIONED in my former letters, the encampment continued here near seven months, the movements and conditions of it, remained very much the same as nothing of much consequence occurred during the time, to disturb or change the daily monotony. There were occasionally during this season, some alarms of the approach of the enemy, which threw the officers and soldiers into active preparations to be prepared to receive them, and in some few instances a part of them went out to meet them, but they all turned out to be without foundation. They also had the effect of producing much fear and consternation among the people. Such was the state of both contending powers at this juncture of time, that neither of them felt much disposition to engage in an attack upon the other, and they remained quiet in their respective positions.

After passing through the winter, less fuel and clothing were necessary, and through the efforts of Congress, and the persevering enterprise of many of the officers of the army, the Commissary Department was better supplied with provisions and other military stores, so that the suffering of the soldiers was, in some measure, mitigated.

The people, as already noticed, suffered severe losses on account of their hay, grain, fodder, horses, cattle, swine, poultry, and in fact almost everything they had, being taken for the use of the army. The property thus taken from them by officers acting under the authority of the superior officers of the army, they were paid for, either by certificates upon the Continental Congress, or in the Continental money of the day. The latter soon died in the hands of many of them, and ended in a total loss.

THE HANGING OF A SPY

During the time of this campaign, a person, I think from the city of Philadelphia, was found in the camp acting in the capacity of a spy for the enemy, and he was very summarily tried and executed by a military tribunal. The place where the gallows, on which he was hanged, stood was shown to me about twenty-five years ago, by an old man whom I overtook on the road near the place. He was a stranger to me. His residence, he said, was at

Pittsgrove, in the state of New Jersey, that he was a private in Potter's brigade, and had been encamped there, and had witnessed the execution; he also mentioned the name of the individual who had been the victim. I had previously heard of a person of that name being executed as a spy during the time, and the place had been pointed out to me, which was the identical one mentioned by the old man I met with, and I could not but admire his retentive memory, that after a lapse of forty-seven years, he could so clearly point out the place of its location. This circumstance, together with other things that he related to me at the time, fully satisfied me that he had been one of the number encamped there, and one that had suffered severely at the time, and was entitled to a pension, that he was then endeavoring to obtain.

To satisfy myself more fully on this head, I lately made inquiry of my aunt, now the only one of the family living that witnessed the time, and who well remembers the passing events of that day, and she fully confirmed the account given me by the old man. She informed me that she well remembers the day of the execution, and of seeing the gallows with a portion of the rope upon it, which remained there for a considerable time after the departure of the army, and that she was often at the place while it stood there. It was erected on the land of David Stephens, a little north of the Gulf Road, near the corner of a piece of land known by the name, "The Fifty Acres," being near the corner of the line between Chester and Montgomery counties. The land on which it stood now belongs to William Henry. I have purposely omitted giving the name of the individual who was executed, as there are many of the same name living in various parts of the country, within the circle of my acquaintance, but I cannot say whether any of them are connected with him or not. I have, therefore, avoided giving it to the public, but have furnished the printers with it.

A DUEL

While the army remained here, a duel took place, between a Lieutenant Green, from New England, and an officer from the South, whose name and rank I have now forgotten. What it was that led to the rash and foolish act I have never understood. The place of meeting was about a quarter of a mile northeast of where the gallows stood, on land then belonging to John Moore. In the engagement Greene was wounded, and died soon after, and was buried at the Friends' burial ground, at the Valley Meeting-house, with the honors of war (so called). My aunt, the venerable Elizabeth Reese, the person just noticed, now in the 82nd year of her age, says she well remembers seeing the procession passing through their orchard, a little north of the house, with muffled drums, and moving slowly to the tune of the dead march. A blanket had been procured in the neighborhood, in which his remains were wrapt, and thus consigned to the grave.

I have heard my grandmother say that after his death, request was made of her for a sheet to bury him in, but such was her stript condition, that she could not comply with their request. They then called on a woman named Mary Pugh, from whom they obtained the blanket. Twenty-eight years after, in digging a grave at the place, his bones were disinterred. The blanket in which they had been wrapped, when discovered, appeared in a state of preservation, but on coming to the air it fell to pieces. I saw the bones soon after they were discovered, and well remember the soundness of the teeth; the blanket I did not see, but was informed of the circumstances, and whose bones they were, by Isaac Walker, a man of unblemished character and reputation, who had charge of the graveyard at the time, and who resided near the place at the time of the interment, and who was always renowned for correct observations and retentive memory.

SOME ADDENDA

I shall now make some addition to the former accounts, the information having been recently obtained, and which would more properly belong to my eighth and eleventh letters. In my eighth, I mentioned never having met with any account of General Wheedon in any accounts of the Revolutionary War, or American biography. A few days since, I found in the Pineville library, a work entitled, "Washington and the Generals of the Revolution," in which there is a short notice of him, the whole of which is contained in about twenty lines duodecimo pages, and taken from the notes of an English traveler, made about the commencement of the Revolution, who speaks of having lodged at his tavern. The account given concerning him there, I do not think fully correct. He calls him George Wheedon. His name, I always understood, was Joseph Wheedon, and the cause of his resigning his office and returning home, is differently stated from what I have always heard it stated from correct information.

In my eleventh letter, some mention was made of officers being quartered at the houses of Samuel Jones and Samuel Richard, but could not give positive information concerning them. In the library at Pineville, I also met with a history of the War of Independence, in which is an engraved map of the encampment at Valley Forge. The outlines of the encampment, the fortifications and breastworks, the courses of the river and stream, and many other things are correctly laid down; but the plan of the arrangement of the different positions, and the quarters of the general officers, are not at all as I have heard them represented by persons who had every means in their power to obtain correct information at the time, and the most of them from actual knowledge. In that map, Generals Woodford, Scott, Clever, Sernea, and Patterson, are represented as stationed on the front line. I never heard of the last three being quartered, or the brigades under their command stationed anywhere in the neighborhood, but still they may have been. The two first I now remember, upon seeing their positions laid down upon the map, to have heard that these were the officers that were quartered at the houses of Samuel Jones and Samuel Richards, Woodward at the latter, and Scott at the former place, which is now occupied as a hotel, known by the name of Keugel's Tavern, on the State Road, leading from New Hope, through Doylestown, Norristown, and West Chester to the Maryland line, about six miles from Norristown and between two and three miles from Valley Forge. I now have a perfect recollection of the two last mentioned officers being quartered at these places, the relation having been given me by a daughter of the said Samuel Richards, the late Elizabeth Walker, who died about sixteen months ago, in the 84th year of her age.

In my next I shall give you an account of some persons who were here during the time of the campaign, who have since filled some very important and conspicuous stations in the history of our country, and discharged important trusts and filled high offices in government, and some other matters, that may be of interest to at least some of my readers.

LETTER XVII

"BENEVOLENT FEMALES"

N THIS letter I hope to bring to a conclusion the greater part of the account I shall give of the encampment. Much more might be added, as I have heard many other things related that would be worthy of notice, particularly the kindness and compassion with which the poor soldiers were treated, by many of the inhabitants of the neighborhood—how they were often supplied with food and other necessaries by the charity of the people, and their wants administered to as far as ability was afforded. If necessary I could give the names of many benevolent females, at the houses of whom some of the general officers were quartered, preparing for the hungry guards, after exposure during the night, a comfortable breakfast in the morning, and furnishing them with stockings and other necessary articles, in their tried situations, to protect them from the cold; but to particularize them and their charitable acts would exceed the limits of the design I had in view in the commencement of the work. I shall, therefore, pass by the most of them. Among them there are a few that I shall slightly notice. These are Sarah Walker, Elizabeth Stephens, Priscilla Stephens, Margaret Beaver, Elizabeth Moore and Jane Moore. The two first were dead before my time; the four last all died between the years 1812 and 1820. I mention these not because there were no others worthy of a place or notice here, but merely to inform my readers that I once remember to have seen the four last meet together, about thirty years after the campaign, and although they fought not their "battles o'er again," yet they found much exercise for their conversational powers in discoursing of the events at the time of the campaign; and although nearly forty years have elapsed since that time, yet the lively interest I took in listening to them is still fresh in my memory.

LATER CELEBRITIES

I shall now proceed to give some notice of persons who were here during the time, who have since risen to eminence in political affairs, and filled important offices in civil government. The biographies of many of these are too well known to need a repetition in a work like this. The account of them will, therefore, be very brief.

Among these were two persons, who, on account of the important stations they have since filled, and some other circumstances known to most of the American people, which have rendered them very notorious, viz., the death of the one, and the subsequent dishonorable life and neglected death of the other; on this account these two individuals will be first noticed. These were Alexander Hamilton and Aaron Burr—the former one of the aids of the Commander-in-Chief, and his reputed privy counsellor; the latter commanded a regiment attached to General Varnum's brigade.

Of those that were there, a few only among the many can be enumerated: among these were Colonel Trumbull, more generally known as one of the first historical painters in the United States. He was also one of the aids of the Commander-in-Chief; and, with Hamilton and others, stationed near or at Headquarters; Timothy Pickering, since extensively known in the National Cabinet and House of Representatives; George Clinton, since Vice President of the United States; Henry Dearborn, Secretary of War during the administration of Thomas Jefferson, and Commander-in-Chief of the army at the commencement of the War of 1812, and since minister to Portugal; Joseph Hiester, Governor of Pennsylvania, elected in the year 1820; Richard Peters, District Judge of the United States Court for the district of Pennsylvania; Thomas Forrest, a member of Congress for the city and county of Philadelphia, in the Seventeenth and Eighteenth Congresses; Thomas Blount, of North Carolina, a member of Congress, elected to a seat in the House during the early part of the administration of Washington, and successively re-elected during the administrations of Adams, Jefferson, and Madison, until the time of his death, which occurred at Washington during the early part of the year 1812; and many others whose names I might mention, and others that I have forgotten; and, therefore, let them pass without any further observation.

In noticing the names of the above persons, commissioned officers of the army only were taken in view.

Among the privates there were no doubt many who have since risen to eminence in public life, who were unknown even by name to many of the inhabitants of the place. But there was one individual, who was here as a private soldier, in the infantry, suffering, in common with his companions in arms, all the hardships and deprivations that have been so often described, who has since risen to one of the highest gifts in the power of the Chief Magistrate of the nation to bestow. I mean John Marshall, late Chief Justice of the United States.

I was once informed by John Moore, who owned the land on which the fort bearing his name was erected, and who always resided on the same farm, and at the time of the campaign must have been more than twenty-one years of age, that during the

THE HISTORY OF VALLEY FORGE 85

time James Madison, since President of the United States, was there a private in a troop of cavalry, that he had often seen him during the time. Not having in my possession any biography of James Madison, and having no recollection of ever having in all the accounts I have read of him, seen any mention made of his having, at any time during the contest, entered the service of the Continental Army, I do not state this as a positive fact. My informant was a man of credibility, but he might have been mistaken in regard to the person. I heard him mention the circumstance during the canvass of the Presidential election of 1812, between James Madison and Dewitt Clinton.

Having now noticed many of the incidents of that interesting period, in former numbers, I may here be allowed to introduce a few more additional remarks concerning the encampment, which ought more properly to have claimed notice in some former letters, but were inadvertently omitted. These are a further description of the fortifications and an occount of some of the public buildings that were erected and used for the army; a view of the face of the country, as I have heard it represented at the time of its being taken possession of for the use of the army, and the state it was left in on their removal.

THE FORTS

The breastworks have been described. The forts were formed by making large embankments of earth, by digging a trench about eight feet wide and four feet deep, the earth excavated in the process forming the embankment. The forts called Moore's Forts on the northeast extremity, were enclosed by three mounds, on four sides, with a small exception on the northwest side, which was left open for egress. A fort erected near the house of David Stephens, was constructed on a similar plan, except that the place of egress was on the southeast side. Those that were surrounded by embankments on every side, or nearly so, were in the form of a trapezium, having the longest line on the side from which they had most reason to expect an attack from the enemy. The average length of the lines, or mounds enclosing them, I should suppose varied from ten to sixteen feet in length. The other forts were all erected in the same way, except that, if I rightly recollect, they were enclosed only on three sides, except those in the centre, which were more strongly entrenched by embankments on every side. The forts known as John Moore's Fort and David Stephen's Fort, near his residence, were placed on eminences from which a view of the surrounding country on both sides of the river could be commanded, and they be used to prevent the enemy crossing the river. The former could also be used to check the progress of an attack on the same side of the river it was constructed. Mordecai Moore's Fort could be used on similar occasions, but it chiefly commanded a view of that portion of country, from which the most danger of an attack was contemplated, as it lay nearest the city of Philadelphia, where the enemy were then encamped. The others on the Rear Line, and one near the termination of the breastwork on the Front Line, to be used in case of an attack by a circuitous route. In addition to these, there were a few others in the centre used as magazines, and intended as places to retreat to, as the last means of defense, should they be found necessary.

BAKE-HOUSE AND ARMORY

A public bake-house was established at Valley Forge, in the house now occupied by the proprietor, for the use of the army; but this was insufficient to supply the whole demand, and many poor families in the neighborhood of the encampment earned their bread by baking for the soldiers and some officers, not in the vicinity of the bake-house.

A temporary armory was erected on the west side of the Valley Creek, at Valley Forge, and used for the purpose of making and repairing arms for the use of the army, but I never heard of it being used for that purpose by the Continental troops after their departure from the place. It stood near the site of the old knitting mill.

I shall now conclude this letter, by observing that in my next I shall give the account, as promised, of the appearance of the face of the country, at the time of their taking possession of it, and some other subjects that occurred at the time.

LETTER XVIII

PROVISION STORE

HE LINES of the encampment did not extend to the westward of the Valley Forge a great distance, not exceeding a mile; as little danger was felt of an attack from that quarter. At the house of a person named Frederic Geerhart, near the western line, a general depository or provision store for the use of the army, was established. My father, during the most of the campaign, had the charge or superintendency of it. Similar ones may have been established in other places, but I have no recollection of ever hearing of any of them particularly designated. It was in depositories of this kind that the provisions for the use of the army, whenever, as was seldom the case, were more than sufficient for the immediate use of the army, were placed, to be delivered out as necessity required in rations to the troops for their support.

BEFORE AND AFTER

The whole of the country embraced in the lines of the encampment, on both sides of the Valley Creek, and some portion of country lying in the Great Valley, on the eastern side of the Front Line Hill, at the time of the arrival of the army, was either a dense forest of heavy timber, or highly cultivated farms. As regards the state of agriculture in that day, an extensive business in the manufacture of bar iron and flour for exportation had been carried on at Valley Forge, and that portion of country lying in the Great Valley, being of a highly productive nature, and owned by Thomas Waters, Abijah Stephens, Benjamin Jones, Jacob Walker, John Beaver and Joseph Walker, in Chester county, and Mordecai Moore and John Moore, in Montgomery county, teemed with the flocks and herds, and produced abundantly of the real necessaries of life, which were the chief objects of agriculture of that day; the buildings and improvements on them good, substantial and commodious, for that early day, when luxury and false show and splendor had not usurped the place of real comfort and convenience. But upon their departure, a far different appearance in the face of the country, presented itself. The stately forests, consisting of the venerable oak, the majestic hickory, and numerous other trees, beautiful, young and thrifty, were promiscuously cut down, the fences used for the enclosures taken away, for fuel, or, as before noticed, used in the construction of huts or forming pickets. The flocks and herds, lately so abundant upon them, all taken for the use of the army. At the Valley Forge, the sound of the hammer was no longer heard in manufacturing iron; the naked walls of the buildings, lately used for the purpose, were all that remained to remind observers of the business lately conducted there. It is true, all the buildings on the property of other persons in the vicinity of the encampment, were not destroyed. The enemy and our own troops had not burned or in no other way destroyed any of them, but the people had been, in consequence of the peculiar situation in which they had been placed, and tried state of the army, had been deprived of almost all the necessaries of life in addition to their lands being thus laid waste. So that the country then presented nothing but the picture of wasting and destruction. I cannot, of course, remember that period of time, but while writing these things, my mind is carried back in retrospection to the times alluded to, they bring afresh to my memory, what I have so often heard repeated concerning them, that I sometimes almost fancy I lived in that day, and that I have actually beheld the scenes I have endeavored to present to my readers.

THE BRITISH INFORMED

In my next I shall have some further allusions to the subject. The remainder of this I wish to devote to some matters that occurred near the close of the campaign, and particularly to a circumstance that occurred about that time, that I have never seen any account of, that shows that the movements of the Continental Army were either very closely and secretly watched, or that the fidelity of some of the superior officers was not to be fully trusted to. I have often heard my father relate the circumstance, and as he belonged to the army, and was well acquainted with all its movements, I publish it, probably for the first time, upon that authenticity, and endeavor to give it as nearly as possible as I have heard it related by him. In giving this account, it will be necessary to take some notice of the British army, under command of General Howe.

After the battle of Germantown, and the passage of their fleet up the Delaware to Philadelphia, they were left in absolute possession of the city, where they entered in triumph to take up their winter quarters, enjoying every luxury and abundance even to excess, as their sovereign, in whose service they were engaged, furnished them liberally with the means of gratifying the vain mind. While Washington and his army were at Valley Forge, suffering all the accumulated miseries, hardships and privations that have been mentioned, many of them barely sheltered from the inclement storms by the miserable huts they dwelt in, the enemy were dwelling secure in their comfortable houses, and though frequently feeling inconvenience for the want of fuel, yet they were well fed and well clothed; and, if not marrying and giving in marriage, they were eating and drinking, rioting and feasting, enjoying their parties of pleasure, attending balls and visiting theatres, and various other amusements. And to crown the whole, towards the close of the campaign, when Gen. Howe was about to leave the country and return to England, the officers resolved to honor him by a splendid pageantry or fete called the Merchianza, for a full description of which my readers are referred to Watson's Annals of Philadelphia, and Sherman Day's Historical Researches of Pennsylvania, under the head of "Philadelphia," where they will find a very graphic description given of it. [It may here be noticed that I saw about two years ago (1848) in the possession of John F. Watson, of Germantown, one of the original cards of invitation to this splendid fete.]

Through their long and uninterrupted course of selfish pleasure, thinking themselves secure from danger, they had become rather careless about guarding their outposts from surprise. Washington thinking this a very suitable time, to make an attack upon some of these stationed near the Wissahickon, between Germantown and the Schuylkill, hoping by a manoeuvre of this kind to partially weaken some of their forces, and to secure some of their stores, arms, ammunition and artillery. In order that the utmost secrecy might be observed, he called a council of officers, at 12 o'clock at night, at Headquarters. Of whom this council consisted, I have never fully understood, but Generals Lee and Knox and Col. Hamilton, together with a few others constituted it. The result of the conference was that they agreed that on the next day, a detachment of the army was to march from the encampment, across the river Schuylkill, at Matson's Ford, opposite Conshohocken, and fall upon the outposts early in the morning of the second day after the consultation. The plan being thus arranged, it was supposed to be only known to the officers who were present at the conference, and upon whom the utmost secrecy was enjoined, until the commencement of the march.

Preparations were made to carry the attack into effect, and though they had every reason to believe their movements were known only to the aforesaid officers who were charged with the execution of it, yet Washington with that caution that always characterized him, was unwilling to allow the main body to proceed, without sending in advance a small body of men to reconnoitre the country and if possible, to discover whether any of the enemy were lying in ambush or on their way to meet them. This party upon arriving on an eminence, upon the Gulf Road, near the house of John Hughes, from which place, there is a distinct view of Barren Hill, discovered a body of the British army marching out to meet them, and it was ascertained they lay in ambush near the Schuylkill, in order that when our troops were crossing the river, which they meant to wade, it not being more than three feet deep, attack them at the time, when owing to the disadvantages in which they would be placed, they would have been easily subdued. It was evident that the enemy had notice of their intended movement, but in what way it was conveyed has never and, in all probability, never will be known. Whether some person, like Lydia Darrah, was listening to the officers while in secret conclave, and conveyed the intelligence, or whether some of the officers proved treacherous, and being in league with some of the disaffected Tories of that day, some of whom were ever ready, through the love of British gold, to act as messengers and thus convey intelligence to the enemy, must always be a matter of conjecture. I could give my father's opinion, but think best to forbear for the present. The prudence and precaution of Washington frustrated their object. The American army, after commencing their march, received the information from the body of men sent in advance, and they all returned to camp.

I shall now take leave of the transactions of the army at the encampment, and in my next give an account of their departure.

LETTER XIX

DEPARTURE AND DESOLATION

N COMMENCING this communication, I shall commence with the departure of the army from the place; this occurred in the fore part of the summer of 1778. The same caution that had rendered it necessary upon their arrival to conduct their marches with as much secrecy as possible, was as essential at the time of their departure, and little or no notice was given to the main body of the army, or to the inhabitants of the vicinity, of their removal, previous to the morning of their march. The British having evacuated Philadelphia, our troops took possession of it the same day. Leaving the encampment at Valley Forge was so unexpected to the soldiers that I was once informed by a woman who baked for the army, that she had received from the soldiers her usual supply of flour, to be baked for them on the day of their departure, all of which were left on her hands, furnishing her and her family with an unexpected and welcome supply of the staff of life. I have also heard it related, that soon after their departure, there was found in the camp, by persons whom curiosity had led to visit the place, in huts where baking and other culinary operations were performed, batches of dough left in an unbaked state, on account of their sudden march; and also many other utensils, such as camp kettles, cabooses (one of which I believe is in our family at this time), axes, canteens, and numerous other articles that could not be collected or taken off, in the hurry of the occasion.

It was a very common thing, since my recollection, to find on the ground some memento of that period. I have often, in company with my elder brothers and other boys, sometimes with grown persons, generally strangers, who, when in the neighborhood, had a curiosity to visit the place, and sometimes alone have I spent hours in traversing the ground in search of these relics of the Revolution—not that they were of any great value, but to possess them as curiosities to remind us of that period. There is even at the present day, sometimes an occasional relic of that day turned up by the ploughshare.

But I am digressing from the subject of their departure, and must return to it; and by introducing a fanciful view of the time and place, endeavor to show my readers the distressed situation and appearance of the place. I must request them, in idea at least, to accompany me to the neighborhood of the place and the scenes I have been describing. Let us fancy ourselves arrived there, and in imagination let us consider it to be in the midsummer of 1778, and that we are standing on Mordecai Moore's fort, from which, in every direction that we turn our eyes, on both sides of the Schuylkill, we behold from this eminence, particularly on the western side in the Great Valley, a portion of country excelled by very few, if any, in fertility, in the state of Pennsylvania, and lately fruitful as the rich land of Goshen, and beautiful to look upon as the well watered plains of Jordan, and, if rightly improved, would produce abundance. But all around is nothing but desolation—the fields are destitute of vegetation, and the lands, once so highly productive, lie uncultivated and without enclosure. The trees of the forest are all cut down, and nothing but the stumps left remaining; wasting destruction and devastation are apparent wherever we turn our eyes on that side of the river. This gloomy prospect leads us to enquire, Why are these things so?

Let us now imagine that we fall in company with some of the Moores, and Walkers, or Stephenses, or other of the worthies of that day, who from severe experience had known the causes that had produced these effects; and they would inform us in answer to our questions, that they were produced from the war they were then engaged in; and the desolation we everywhere behold around us was produced by the encampment at that place, that these were the effects of it. They would explain to us the use of the fortifications and redoubts, and show us the pickets, then, pointing to the south and west, would show us the miserable huts that were hastily erected to shelter the poor, famished and suffering soldiers from the inclement storms of the preceding winter; and directing our attention to the place lately abounding with the lofty, towering oaks and other stately forest trees, and to their fertile lands, now lying a common; they would tell us their timber was cut down, and their fences taken to construct huts and pickets and to furnish fuel for the soldiers, to protect and preserve them from the cold chilling wind and driving snow. It is thus they would inform us of the causes that had thus laid waste that fair portion of country; and at the same time relate to us many interesting anecdotes of that period, which have never been published. They would ask us to accompany them to Valley Forge, and there they would point to us the same feature of desolation, though not the same fertility of soil, all lying waste; they would show us the naked walls of the buildings, lately burned by the enemy, and tell us that where there is now nothing but gloomy silence, was lately heard the sound of the hammer and the hum of business, and there was seen the hardy laborer busily engaged in manufacturing iron for useful and peaceful purposes; but now all is still, gloomy and death-like. From thence they would conduct us to other parts of the ground occupied by the encampment; and, in all our rambles, the same evidence of desolation would be still apparent everywhere in the course of the journey—for the fruitful field had become desolate; and the garden a waste place. But while showing to us the dreary state of things, and, though for the present discouraged under the prospect of things and the state of affairs, yet they would express a hope of the return of better days, when their waste places should through industry be again restored, and their gardens now desolate should blossom as the rose, and peace return like the dove bearing the olive branch and be again restored in our borders.

I shall now leave this imaginary scene, which has been introduced as a picture to show the state of the place, after the army had removed from there, and that I might in some of my future numbers contrast it with its present appearance. I shall proceed to remark, that it is not my intention to pursue the movements of the army any further after leaving the place, my object being to give, as nearly as I possibly can, a history of the Valley Forge, as promised in my first letter. The movements and condition of the army after leaving that place has, therefore, very little if anything further to do with the subject. Those that wish further information on that head are referred to the history of the Revolution. Neither is it necessary for me to dwell much on that period of time that elapsed between their removal from this place to the final establishment of our independence by the treaty of Amiens, a period of near five years, as nothing of much importance occurred in that time that need require notice. In my next I shall refer to some matters relating to the sufferings of the people, and the huts that were left on the land of different persons in the lines of the encampment, and the difficulties they met with on account of the loss of their property.

A FEW REFLECTIONS

Before I close this account of the departure of the army from the encampment ground, indulge me for a few moments in expressing a few reflections that involuntarily present themselves. In contemplating that interesting period of time when the army was encamped here, and reflecting on the number that composed it, a query very naturally arises of this kind—Where are they now? Since that period seventy-two years have passed away; and taking into view that the most of them must have been more than twenty years of age, it must appear evident that very few if any of them are now (1850) in mutability; if there be any remaining, they have advanced to that age that they are becoming strangers in the midst of a new succession of men. And if it be not the case now, it will be in a very short time, that there will be none left to tell us of these things that they have witnessed and I have endeavored to describe. Among the circle of my acquaintance, which is by no means limited, I now know of none of that portion living. And during a residence of more than twenty-two years in Bucks county, I never met but three persons who formed a part of that body, and these have descended to the grave in a good old age. Their names were Samuel Smith, Andrew Dennison and James Kirk—the two first well known to many of my readers. An expression made use of by the venerable Andrew Dennison the last time I ever saw him may be with propriety inserted in this place; the day was cold and windy, the ground covered with snow, when I overtook him in the road near Forestville and gave him a seat in the sleigh to ride with us. Upon some remarks upon the inclemency of the weather, he replied: "The people of the present day know nothing about cold; if the young men of the present day, with all the advantages they possess, had to pass through what I and my fellow soldiers passed through at Valley Forge, the very thoughts of it would make them quail." There may have been during the time of my residence here, many of these patriots living, but I never to my knowledge met with them; there may still be, but I know them not.

Of those who have been alluded to who have paid the debt of nature, and who were among the number who shared the severe sufferings of the camp, it is an instructive and interesting engagement to contemplate the subsequent history of their lives. Among those who survived the war and returned to their families and friends, could it be possible for us to ascertain fully their future lives, we would see some among them rising to eminent stations in civil government, others in commercial, mercantile, agricultural and mechanical operations, that have risen to wealth, eminence and respectability; some who, in the various and devious paths of literature, have shone conspicuous and become ornaments to their country and a blessing to civil and religious society. We look upon the lives of those with a pleasing satisfaction, and may feel justly proud of and thankful for our free and liberal government, which gives to all an equal opportunity to eminence in the world, and fulfil our duties as members of this great and growing republic. But while we enjoy this fond view, there is cause of deep regret, when we also reflect that there are many others of them who were blessed with talents and abilities to have rendered themselves equally eminent and useful and to have made them if not equally opulent, at least wholly respectable, who have through low and debasing habits, to which they have given way, lost their standing in society, glided down the streams of intemperance and insignificance, and been buried in the gulf of oblivion. But while we regret their infirmities, let us draw a veil over their frailties, and leave them to repose.

LETTER XX

A COMMUNITY PROSTRATE

IN MY LAST, the army had left the encampment, and I had endeavored to represent in as clear a manner as possible the dreary state of the neighborhood after their removal; but the state of things can be better imagined than described. Language would fail to give anything like an adequate idea of it, as I have heard it often represented by persons who had learned and known the then state of things by experience. I may here remark that while all parts lying contiguous suffered from the effects in a greater or less degree, that part of it lying on the south and east of the Front Line Hill suffered most severely. The greater part of the men were stationed there, and their destitute condition placed them in a situation, in which to obtain fuel and provisions necessary forced them to observe the old adage concerning it, viz., that "necessity knows no law"; and acting under the impulse of it, the country was soon cleared of all the timber, rails, provisions, and all other things they could possibly obtain.

Among those who suffered most severely was my grandfather —in truth this calamity fell heavily upon him. His timber, as before noticed, was all cut down and carried off the premises, either for fuel or constructing of huts, and all the rails on his farm of more than two hundred acres were used for similar purposes. Very few huts were erected on his premises, it lying principally on the south of the Front Line Hill. From the destruction of timber and loss of rails and other property none were exempt, all fared alike, no partiality was shown in this respect, except as the general officers quartered at different places exercised in some measure their authority when it was carried to too great an excess in taking things that were used in the different families for domestic purposes. While the army remained here, the people of the place were very much on an equality as regarded their property and living, and the future prospects of overcoming their losses very much the same. As the prospect was a very dreary one, they all concluded that their timber and rails were all destroyed, and difficulties would have to be surmounted before their property could be partially restored to its former condition; but after the removal of the army, some felt the effects of it more than others. The huts which had been erected for the use of the army remained on the premises after their departure, and the rails forming the pickets were left there. As noticed in a former communication, the huts and pickets were principally on the farms of Mordecai Moore and David Stephens; the rails left in the pickets answered for fencing, and the timber of which the huts were constructed answered for purpose of fuel and rail. These two men had suffered in common with others the loss of timber and the destruction of fences, but owing to the circumstances of the huts and pickets being left on their premises, they did not feel the loss of their timber to so great an extent as some others. The farms of Thomas Waters, Joseph Walker, Benjamin Jones, John Bean and others lying on the southeast of the encampment being further from the main body of the army, I have understood suffered not so severely from the effects of the encampment, as the owners of the land had timber land in other places that escaped the ravages of the army, so they had to supply them with fencing and fuel. But this was not the case with my grandfather, he had none of these means to resort to. His only dependence for fuel was the few huts that were left standing on his premises. Unlike some others, he had no timber land that escaped destruction to resort to for fencing; he was thus placed under the necessity of purchasing and hauling from a considerable distance rails to enclose his land, and also buy all the horses and a great deal of other stock for conducting farming operations, and having in common with others, lost the greater part of his movable property and household goods during the encampment, particularly in the early part of it, as mentioned in former communications. All these things had to be provided for the family, which required much expense and labor, so that his situation was truly a very trying one, from the effects of which he had never fully recovered during the remainder of his days. It is true he received from the government some remuneration for the damages sustained, but it was in Continental money, which soon depreciated and was eventually repudiated, so that the whole may be said to have ended in a total loss.

THE GERMAN PHYSICIAN AND THE RIDING HORSE

I may here mention without too much digression a circumstance that shows how little regard was paid to the rights of another in regard to property, by some of the persons connected with the army. My grandfather in the early part of the campaign had all his horses taken from him except one, a favorite riding horse which he had occasion to use frequently, as he was much engaged both in the camp and the surrounding country as a surgeon, or healer of fractures, ulcers of various kinds, dislocations and other similar maladies and casualties. On this account this horse was never taken or used by any of the officers or men. On the morning of the departure of the army, a German physician, who had spent a considerable portion of time with Dubryson, took the horse by stealth, called at a house near the place, borrowed a saddle, and informed the person he obtained it of, that he had borrowed the horse of Doctor Stephens (as he called him) to ride to the ferry at Philadelphia, and would return with him in the evening or the morning of the following day. He never returned with horse or saddle, and thus my grandfather's last horse was taken from him.

FROM WAR TO PEACE

The peculiar situation of the country at this time, and the losses the people had sustained continued to oppress them not only during the remainder of the war but for several years after, so that little progress was made by many of them to resuscitate their desolated farms, and the iron manufacturing business at Valley Forge was during the residue of the war suspended. The owners of the farms thus laid waste generally continued to reside upon them during the remainder of the war. David Stephens, soon after the removal of the army, with his wife and some other branches of the family, moved to Nantmeal, in Chester county, and continued there some years. The mansion that had been occupied by Colonel Dewees at Valley Forge, having been burned, he with his family removed to a house of his father-in-law in the Valley, the place where Gen. Mifflin had been quartered, at which place he continued to reside for several years, except a small portion of time that he resided in Philadelphia. As I shall take some notice of the most of these persons in a future communication, I shall take no further notice of them at present.

Having noticed many of the principal events of that period in the history of our country, that transpired in the neighborhood of the Valley Forge during that interesting and deeply trying time, though there are yet many things that might be related, I must omit them, as time and many pressing engagements preclude my entering more fully into the subject. I promised my readers in the commencement of the work, to carry it on from its early settlement to the present time (1850). I shall, therefore, now dismiss the consideration of any matters connected with the war of the Revolution, or the campaign at Valley Forge, which have already claimed so much of your attention, only as they may occasionally come in future numbers by way of reference, and in my future letters I shall turn from the gloomy picture of things, from the "lines and tented fields," to that period of time when peace with her olive branch had returned to our borders, when the destructive sword had been exchanged for the ploughshare, and danger and destruction no longer hovered around us. When the Valley Forge had been rebuilt, and instead of confused noise of the camp being heard in its borders, was heard afresh the noise of the hammer in the manufacturing of iron, the most valuable and useful of all mineral substances, when the farms in that fair portion of country, surrounding it on every side, no longer lay waste and unproductive, but through the hand of industry and the blessings of peace, they were again restored, the waste places enclosed, and the fields clothed with plenty for the sustenance of man and beast.

In my next, I shall commence an account of the rebuilding of the Valley Forge, the revival of business at the place, and confining myself exclusively to the original estate as it was at the time of the conclusion of the war, notice its different owners, the changes of manufacturing business at different periods, the improvements it has undergone, its present state, and many other things in connection with the place, the most of which have occurred since my time, and will be generally furnished from actual knowledge and observation.

LETTER XXI

THE FORGE RELIT

N THIS commuication I propose giving an account of the Valley Forge from the termination of the war down to the present time, confining myself as much as possible to the Valley Forge tract of land as it was held at that time, and shall endeavor to present it in as connected a manner as it will admit of. About the time alluded to, another forge was built considerably lower down the stream than the former one that was burned by the British. The present (1850) cotton factory covers the site of the forge last erected. It stood there and was used as a tilt mill until the year 1814. A slitting and rolling mill were erected a few years after the forge, on the opposite side of the stream, in Chester county. These buildings were erected by William Dewees, David Potts and Isaac Potts. The former commenced the manufactory of bar iron, and the place again began to assume the prospect of business being revived. Neither of the others was engaged at that time with him as partners in the manufacturing business. David Potts residing in the city of Philadelphia, where he kept an iron store; and Isaac Potts lived at headquarters—he having the grist mill at the place.

William Dewees, who was very aristocratic, and who moved in a style far above his means to support, in a few years failed, was sold out by the sheriff, which closed his business at the place, and ended his connection with the family. About the year 1792, an assessment of the damage done to the Valley Forge estate by the burning of the different buildings by the enemy, was taken by John Bartholemew and John Davis; and if I recollect right, the amount of valuation was over twelve thousand dollars. William Dewees petitioned Congress at that time for damages he had sustained on the occasion; but owing to the low state of the national treasury at the time, it was not granted. He kept a duplicate of the documents prepared on the occasion, but nothing further was done by him in the business in his life time. The sequel of his life I shall not pursue more than to say that it was marked by a sad reverse of fortune, and he ended his days at an advanced age, near the place in the year 1809. Of the claim I shall speak more in some future number.

The business of the Forge and other iron works, after the failure of William Dewees, was for a few years carried on by

Isaac Potts, during which time a division of the property took place—David Potts taking the iron works and all the land in Chester and Montgomery, lying on the south side of Nutt's road and the Gulf road, and a small part on the north side of the Gulf road in Montgomery, on which the mansion house and some other buildings had been erected, having the privilege of a road or passage from the Gulf road to the river Schulykill and a landing thereon forever, for all articles, flour and wheat and other grain excepted, it being understood between them that no grist or other mill for manufacturing or grinding flour or grain of any kind should be erected on any part of the estate of David Potts. Isaac Potts took the mill and farm on which headquarters stood, lying on the Schuylkill, with the privilege of using the above road or passage to the Gulf road forever, for all articles, iron and charcoal manufactured on the premises only excepted, it being likewise understood that no works of any kind for the manufacture of iron should be erected on the place. The prohibitions have been observed by all subsequent owners of any part of either estate, a clause to that effect being inserted in the deeds of all purchasers since that time, at least all I have ever written or have had in my possession.

THE HEADQUARTERS AFTER THE WAR

As the headquarters of Washington is the most noted place in the vicinity, I shall now proceed with an account of them, detached from any other matter. Isaac Potts continued to reside there, some time after the division of the property. About 1794, if my memory serves me correctly, he sold the property to Jacob Paul of Germantown, in whose family it remained till 1826; it then belonged to his son, Joseph Paul. It was then purchased by an association of people who entertained the visionary idea of establishing a community of mutual interests at the place, on the principles of Robert Owen, of New Lanark, in Scotland. The existence of this project, if it ever existed at all except in imagination or theory, was very brief. The measure proved a complete failure, and the property was taken by James Jones, one of the number, and the only wealthy person among them, who, about two years after removed to the place, and resided in the mansion occupied as headquarters until his death, which occurred about ten years ago (1840) at an advanced age. His family still (1850) resides there. A few years since the old mill, erected prior to the Revolution, and which had escaped the ravages of that period, was destroyed by fire, communicated by sparks from the locomotive on the Reading Railroad, that passes near it. The mansion is still standing, having undergone very little alteration. It has been often visited by strangers and others, on account of its connection with the Revolution, some of whom I have conducted

The Quarters of the Patriotic Order Sons of America

at Valley Forge, which organization saved to the State Washington's Headquarters, the nucleus of the Park. The pillar of stones to the right is said to be a corner of the Joseph Mann house, where Gen. McIntosh was quartered. See pages 58 and 59.

The Quarters of Geo. Varnum

and now the Quarters of the Daughters of the American Revolution. See pages 57, 59 and 137.

Gen. Huntingdon's Quarters

The lower part of the residence to the foreground, part of the original house, owned by David Stephens, larger part erected by his son, Squire Maurice Stephens, in 1816. The spring house down back, in the rear, is in two parts, which likely correspond in age with the two parts of the house. Now in the Park and known as the "Shepherd Farm." See pages 57, 71, and 136.

Quarters of the Provost Guard

See pages 57 and 133.

there; and I have often pointed out the place to travelers who have been passing on the public road. There are yet some things remaining about the building to remind the visitors of that interesting period, particularly the secret doors that were planned for the Commander-in-chief to effect an escape in case of an emergency.

THE DISPOSITION OF THE POTTS ESTATE

I shall now proceed to give an account of that part of the estate owned by David Potts. Shortly after the division of the property, he removed to reside there. He soon quit the manufactory of bar iron and the rolling and slitting of iron, and the tilt hammer was substituted instead. While he abode there, he disposed of some parts of it lying in Chester county, the greater part of his land being there. At the time of his death, he owned more than eight hundred acres of land, more than seven hundred of it being woodland, young and thrifty, having nearly all grown up since the Revolution. He died in the year 1798, and the property was held by some of his family until the year 1806, the business being conducted by his son-in-law, Reese Brooke, and his son, James Potts. In that year it was sold to Ralph Peacock of Philadeluhia, who held it and conducted the business there between two and three years, when he disposed of it to Jacob Vodges of Philadelphia, who took possession of it sometime during the summer of 1802 (There is some discrepancy here.—Ed.) and held it about six years. From the death of David Potts until purchased by Jacob Vodges, no part of the real estate had been sold, except a lot of about fourteen acres, by the heirs of David Potts. During the time it was held by Jacob Vodges, some of the woodland in Montgomery county was sold off in lots to different persons; and five hundred acres of it in Chester county was sold to John Conard and Joseph Barnes, the former of Germantown, the latter of Philadelphia, the latter at the time Prothonotary of the Supreme Court for the Eastern District of Pennsylvania and since Judge of the District Court of Philadelphia, the former at the time Associate Judge of the Circuit Court of the city and county of Philadelphia, subsequently a member of the Fifteenth Congress, Prothonotary of the Eastern District of Pennsylvania (in the room of Mr. Barnes), and Marshal of the Eastern District of the State of Pennsylvania. He now resides in Elkton, in the State of Maryland. His native place was in this county (Bucks), about three miles from Doylestown. They purchased it upon speculation, and soon after sold about four hundred acres of it off in lots of from three to seven acres, the remainder to a person in the neighborhood, thus placing the original tract at that time in the hands of a great many different owners, and this is the situation it is now placed in, and in all probability will always remain so, as

carried on by John Rogers himself, who removed from the city, and took up his residence at Valley Forge. Toward the close of the year 1825, the whole of Valley Forge estate was professed to be purchased by the aforesaid community for the sum of sixty-five thousand dollars, and at the same time they contracted for other properties in the vicinity, to the amount of seventeen thousand more; but they soon found it much easier to purchase than to comply with the conditions on which they professed to purchase. It soon fell to nought, and the whole property, except that comprising the estate known as Headquarters, which has been noticed, was taken back again. John Rogers continued after this short intermission to reside there for several years. He then disposed of the property to a person named Jason Waters from some one of the New England states, who after residing there a few years and the business declining from various causes, he became embarrassed and the property was sold by the sheriff to Charles Rogers, a nephew of John Rogers. The manufacturing business, I think, is now (1850) conducted by an Englishman named Ogden. Charles Rogers now resides there, and being a man of great wealth, and disposed to improve the property, it is now in a fair way of improving in appearance and prosperity. Many new and substantial buildings have been erected by him; among them, on a very elevated point on the Rear Line Hill, is an observatory, furnished with a large telescope, from which an extended view of the surrounding country, in every direction, may be enjoyed, affording to the observer a very beautiful and diversified prospect of the most lovely and interesting scenery in its native grandeur, highly cultivated farms, splendid mansions and commodious farm houses, neat cottages and handsome villages, the navigable river, the railroad thronged with cars, beautiful streams, hills and dales, "fountains and fresh shades" in abundance, till observation is satisfied in passing

"From house to house, and hill to hill,
And contemplation has her fill."

OTHER LAND WEST OF THE CREEK

Having now completed the account of that part of the original tract of the Valley Forge estate that was held by the Potts family at the time of the encampment, I shall next proceed to notice a portion of country lying on the western side of the Valley creek, the most of it embraced in the lines. The most of this at the time of the Revolution belonged to David Potts, and is included in the general description of his property already given. The rest of it was never remarkable for any occurrances during the war that I have ever heard mentioned, neither do I remember to have heard of any of the general officers being quartered in that section. The land is rather hilly and broken, though well watered and having some excellent springs. The quality of the soil is good, and having been mostly held by industrious farmers, they have quietly pursued their peaceful pursuits, the most of them on a limited scale. It was supposed until lately to possess very few, if any, inducements for speculators to enter upon it, as it was not known to contain any valuable mineral substances beneath its surface. In my early days I have heard it said that bituminous coal existed in the hills in that region, and tales were related of its being known by Indians. If there be any, it has never yet been discovered, and probably never will, as geologists never found anything to indicate its existence in that region.

AN INDIAN TALE

Among the Indian tales, I have heard one so directly related, that I shall give it a place here. Frederick Geerhart, mentioned in a former letter, at whose house a general provision store or depository for the use of the army was established, was a blacksmith by trade, and resided there many years previous to the war, and while some Indians continued to dwell in that part of the country. On one occasion an Indian called upon him to have some repairs done to his gun. Not having any coal on hand, he told him he could not do it, assigning that as a reason. The Indian told him that if he would let him have a bag, he would soon procure him some. Being furnished with one, he started off in a southeasterly direction, and returned in a short time with about a bushel of bituminous coal, with which he repaired the gun. The coal was said to be of the same nature and kind of the far famed Virginia coal, formerly so extensively used by blacksmiths. Upon inquiry where he obtained it, and offering him a powerful inducement (a bottle of rum) to show the place, he consented, and took Geerhart to a hole on a hillside, as he used to relate it, not three miles from his house, where the Indian uncovered an opening in the ground of sufficient dimensions to admit a full grown person to crawl in. Upon entering a few feet in the ground, coal was found in abundance. Wood was at that time very plenty, and the owner of the land on which it was found, and of whom Geerhart claimed a fee for showing him the place, said that he did not wish its existence on his property to be known, as he would have nothing to do with it himself, or dispose of it to any other person for the purpose of mining it. The place, if any, has therefore remained a secret. Geerhart soon after the close of the war, removed to the western part of the state of New York, and in a few years died there. My father, to whom he related the account and from whom I received it, never placed full confidence in it. In the year 1830, when the mania for speculation in coal lands, particularly in Schuylkill county, raged to so great an extent, these legendary tales concerning it were again revived, and a few persons, supposing it to exist on their land, commenced searching for it, but all to no profitable purpose—no traces of it were ever discovered, and they soon relinquished the pursuit.

Other discoveries have been made in that section of country; and some small manufacturing establishments have been commenced, which taken in connection with the Reading Railroad and the Schuylkill navigation, have recently considerably altered the state of things among them. Of these things I shall speak more fully in my next letter, and also give some account of a portion of country lying on the eastern side of the river, immediately opposite the Valley Forge estate, and the section of country I have last alluded to, as its contiguity to the encampment ground justly entitles it to a place in these communications.

Baron Steuben Drilling the Continental Army at Valley Forge
he original, by Abbey, adorns the House of Representative at Harrisburg. Reproduced by permissio
—*Copyright by M. G. Abbey, from a Copley Print copywrighted by Curtis an*

The Vaux-Bakewell-Wetherill Mansion

where Washington and Howe were guests of James Vaux on the same day. See pages 107-110. Original house with additions.

Saylor-Francis Home

joining the Wetherill property on the north. The stone barn amid outbuildings used as a hospital. The publisher of this book has induced the G. A. R. to place a marker above the resting place of soldiers buried on the farm.

LETTER XXIII

ACROSS THE RIVER

ON THE eastern side of the Schuylkill, and immediately opposite the encampment ground, is a portion of country which on account of its contiguity to the place, and its connection with it, particularly after the construction of Sullivan's Bridge, I shall give a place in these narratives, as promised at the close of my last letter.

THE PAULING ESTATE

The river at Headquarters makes a great bend. A large tract of land directly opposite the place, bounded on the south and east by the river, at the time of the Revolution, and for many years after, belonged to the Pauling family; and if I mistake not it was first patented by Henry Pauling, the original ancestor of the family, who emigrated to this Province at a very early period of the proprietary government. At the time of the Revolution it belonged to Henry Pauling, the grandfather of Levi Pauling, mentioned in a former letter, who then lived in a mansion near Pauling's Bridge, the same one mentioned in my fifth letter, where my mother arrived at midnight, when returning home from her journey to hunt Jehu. New and commodious buildings had also been erected on the property, immediately opposite Headquarters, and were occupied by Henry Pauling, Esq. These two houses I have understood were the resort of many officers during the time of the encampment; and it is more than probable that some general officers were quartered there; if so, I know not who they were, not having in proper time availed myself of correct information on the subject. It is a rich alluvial soil, almost imperceptibly rising from the river; and for beauty of situation and fertility of soil, is exceeded by none that I know of, lying on either side of the river. Some of the land was held by members of the family till very lately; the last of it was sold since the death of William Pauling, the last surviving son of Henry Pauling, Esq., to the Wetherills, druggists and manufacturers of white lead, in Philadelphia, who have also at different times since the commencement of the war with Great Britain in 1812, purchased large tracts of valuable land in the neighborhood, of which I shall now proceed to give a more general notice, as far as my knowledge extends of their possessions.

When I removed from that part of the country, a little more than twenty-two years ago, the family of Wetherills owned all the land lying on the east side of the river Schuylkill, commencing about a mile below Valley Forge, and extended up the same to the mouth of the Perkiomen Creek—it being more than two miles in extent on the river, excepting the land just mentioned, that then belonged to William Pauling (since purchased by them) and a farm belonging to John Shearer, Esq., and still held by him. Since owned by them, all the property has been much improved by the erection of suitable and commodious buildings of various kinds, adapted to and necessary for the comfortable accommodation and proper management of large and highly productive farms. It may also be noticed, that they had purchased a large and valuable farm on the western side of the Perkiomen Creek, formerly the property of Thomas Vanderslice. In addition to the buildings and improvements just mentioned, they have erected splendid edifices for private summer residences on some of the properties. These things have much improved the appearance of that part of the country; and the most of them being placed in elevated situations, can be seen with advantage from many places of the encampment ground; and when viewed from this distance, and taken in connection with the beautiful scenery, and the variegated landscape, by which it is on all sides accompanied, renders the prospect extremely beautiful and picturesque.

THE MINES NEAR SHANNONVILLE

I shall now give some notice concerning some valuable mineral substances, supposed to exist in the bowels of the earth, in that section of country. It is now near fifty years since a lead mine was opened on or near the Perkiomen, near a place now called Shannonville. It has been since then worked at various times, and by different persons and companies; but I never heard of it being very lucrative, as they all in succession abandoned it previous to the year 1826. About the commencement of that year a person from Cornwall, England, named Sheffield, who professed to have large experience in the business of mining, commenced working them, and was very confident and sanguine of success in the undertaking. He continued business but a short time, and then like his predecessors gave it up. I do not know whether the Wetherills have purchased this property or not; neither do I know whether the business of mining is carried on there at present or not. Recently copper has been discovered in many places, on both sides of the Schuylkill, in the vicinity of the Valley Forge; and considerable business has been done in making preparation for commencing operations in mining for that substance—a more full account of which will be given in some future numbers.

I hope I may be excused if I encroach upon the time and patience of my readers, by giving a more general description of the property belonging to the Wetherills, lying farther down the river, and likewise relating some other accounts in connection with it. It commences on the river, and extends in a northwesterly direction about three-fourths of a mile. There is a gradual ascent from the river to the main buildings, which are erected on the most elevated part of the premises, about two hundred feet above the stream, the mansion fronting upon it. From the rear of the house, the ground gradually descends toward the Perkiomen. I speak of the property as it was the last time I was there, about twenty-four years ago. From this place, particularly about the mansion, one of the most beautiful prospects is afforded to the observer of the surrounding country, that it is possible to conceive. Here may be viewed, not only the greater part of the country occupied as the encampment ground, but in every direction as far as the sight extends, can be enjoyed a view calculated to charm and please. Those who have visited Prospect Hill on the Neshaminy, on the road from Doylestown to Norristown, may form some idea of it.

THE GUESTS OF JAMES VAUX

This property during the time of the Revolution, and while the army was encamped at Valley Forge, belonged to a person named James Vaux, who then resided there. It is remarkable for a circumstance that occurred there, during the time that he mentioned to me, a short time before his death. He said two distinguished persons were guests at his table on the same day—General Washington and General Howe—the former took breakfast with him; and the latter, supper. This occurred the day after the engagement was to have taken place at the White Horse, about two miles from Goshen Meetinghouse, in Chester county, but was prevented by a heavy fall of rain during the night previous. Those who may have read the history of the Revolutionary War, may remember the account. I could write much concerning that event, as I have heard it related by my father, who was one of the number who experienced the effects of it; but as it does not properly belong to these narratives, I shall at this time omit it. But to return to my story. He also informed me that they both lodged at his house—the one on the night previous to his taking breakfast with him, the other on the night subsequent to his taking supper. During the war he maintained as nearly as possible a strictly neutral position, he being a member of the Society of Friends, and his hospitable mansion was open to both contending powers. He sold the property and removed to the city of Philadelphia, where he continued to reside during the remainder of his life, continuing a steadfast member of the religious society to which he was attached, and always exercised his right of suffrage. He died at an advanced age, about twenty-four years ago. Some of his connections still reside in the city, one of whom a few years since was Recorder of the city.

THE BAKEWELL HOUSE AND AUDUBON

I do not know to whom James Vaux sold the property. When I first remember it, it then belonged to a wealthy Englishman named William Bakewell, the person by whom the celebrated Bakewell sheep were first introduced into this country, he importing them from the farm of his brother in England. He died at the place in the year 1820. His family removed to Kentucky shortly after, where one of his daughters had previously resided several years, having married Joseph D. Audubon, the celebrated ornithologist, universally known in literary circles.

A TRAVELER'S ESTIMATE OF THIS SECTION

In shall conclude by mentioning that an English traveler named Robert Sutcliffe, who spent a considerable portion of time in this country, in the years 1804-5 and 6, and kept a narrative of his journey, has given a very graphic description of this property; but as only the initials of the owner's name are given, a stranger would not know it was the same property—though I do not think the picture is much too highly painted. He (Robert Sutcliffe) speaks of accompanying M. R., meaning Matthew Roberts (a brother of the Honorable Jonathan Roberts), to his cousin, W. B.'s, meaning William Bakewell, and proceeds to pass high enconiums upon the farm and appurtenances; should any of my readers see the work, they will there find it more fully described. I might say much more concerning the other places in the parts lying on the eastern side of the river, particularly the Norris Manor, the most of which is still held by branches of the family; but as the most of them, though equally as near the Valley Forge as some as will hereafter be described, yet not being embraced in the lines of the encampment to proceed further with these would exceed the the limits of my original intention.

In my next I shall proceed to that portion of the country lying around Valley Forge, on the east side of the Valley Creek, where the different officers mentioned were quartered.

Quarters of Gen. Maxwell

original building, erroneously referred to as the quarters of Gen. Knox, then owned by John Brown, now owned by U. S. Senator P. C. Knox and known as the Valley Forge Farm. See pages 58 and 111 and also the Preface to the Third Edition of this History.

Quarters of Gen. Lafayette

original building, owned by Samuel Havard, now known as the Harry Wilson farm. See page 112.

Quarters of Gen. Knox

owned by John Havard, long known as the Davis farm, now owned by Thomas Royal. Gen. Duportale was also quartered here, who cut his initials on a door jamb, which a repairing carpenter some years ago regarded as an intrusion on his world and he planed them out. See pages 58 and 112 and Preface to Third Edition.

Quarters of Gen. Lee

owned by David Havard, and years later by his grandson David Havard, now the farm of Col. Cassatt. See page 115.

LETTER XXIV

EAST OF THE VALLEY CREEK

IN THIS I shall commence giving a description of that section of country in Chester and Montgomery counties lying within the limits of the encampment and immediately in their vicinity, where the general officers mentioned in my former letters were quartered. In so doing I shall refer to the persons who owned or occupied them at the time of the encampment, and also have reference to some of their different owners since that period, and the owners of them at the present time, together with some remarks and observations concerning some of the changes they have since passed through, many of which I shall state from actual knowledge, they having mostly taken place since my recollection, particularly the time of the death of the most of the owners and occupants of the places at the time of the Revolution.

THE FARM OF JOHN BROWN

In the first place I shall commence with those on the southwestern boundary, which, at the time, belonged to John Brown, Samuel Havard, John Havard and Samuel Richards. These all live on the south side of the Baptist road, except a portion of the land then belonging to John Brown. At his house Gen. Maxwell was quartered, and on a part of the estate some of the breastworks were thrown up, and a part of it still remains in a tolerably good state of preservation. There were also erected on this property, several forts, the most of which are still remaining visible, and have undergone but little alteration since that time, as they were all on land that has never been cultivated, having been kept for a woodland. These remains of the Revolution are frequently visited by persons who have it within their power and feel an interest in these things. He continued to reside there the remainder of his days. His farm was large and very productive, being in the rich Valley of Chester county. By strict economy and persevering industry, he became very wealthy, lived to an old age, and died in the year 1823. The farm previous to his death had been divided into two farms, both at this time sufficiently large. They are now owned, the original mansion place by his daughter, the other by his daughter-in-law, widow of his only son. It belongs to her during her life time, and then descends to her children. There is now none of his male descendants left of the same name.

THE FARM OF SAMUEL HAVARD

Lafayette was quartered at the house of Samuel Havard. This farm joined John Brown's on the south, and lay a little beyond the lines of the encampment. It was held by him during his life time. He was a very wealthy man, lived and died unmarried. His death occurred in the year 1808, leaving all the property, with a very small exception, both real and personal, to a grandson of his brother. This caused much dissatisfaction among other and nearer relations of his, and after many years and much money were spent in litigation, the will was finally established, and the legatee placed in peaceable possession of the property. He soon after relinquished his profession as a physician in which he was previously fast rising into eminence, and entered into a career of land speculation, which soon dissipated the property, and the real estate was sold to John Sharpless of Delaware county, who held it for several years, being occupied by his son-in-law. Since the death of John Sharpless the property was sold. It is now owned by John Worthington and David Wilson. It is divided into two farms, each containing more than eighty acres. John Worthington occupied the farm and mansion house in which Lafayette resided. The house having, the last time I saw it, undergone but very little change since that time.

THE FARM OF JOHN HAVARD

The farm of John Havard, at whose house Knox was quartered, adjoining the latter one, is situated on the State road, from New Hope to the Maryland line, and extends towards the Valley Forge, on both sides of the Baptist road. That portion lying on the northeast of the latter road was in the lines of the encampment, upon which many lines are still visible. He died before my time, and I never remember to have understood the time. He left one daughter. She married a man named William Davis. They lived during their life times upon it. Their deaths occurred within five weeks of each other; not quite two years ago. Some of their children still reside there and own the property. The eastern extremity of this place was the extent of the picket guard in that direction. The remains of a chimney stood there for many years after, even since my remembrance, it was called the stone picket, and it is sometimes designated by that name even at this time, when all traces of it are obliterated. William Davis at the time of his death, was about eighty-two years of age, being one of the last survivors of that period, who retained a lively recollection of the time of the encampment. He possessed a good memory, and retained his bodily and mental powers, to the close of life. I regret not having availed myself of more information that he might have given me on these subjects. I may, at this place, notice an account he gave me about twenty-six years ago, which exhibits acute observation and strength of memory. He was at work in his barn, and observed a person at some distance, coming toward the house. He told some persons who were engaged with him, that he, calling him at the same time by his name, was a person who was a sergeant in the army, and who used to be at his father's during the Revolution, and whom he had not seen since that time. This was correct. He had, after a lapse of nearly half a century, returned to the place to seek for some person to enable him to prove his services in the army, to entitle him to a pension.

RICHARDS AND JONES FARMS

The farms of Samuel Richards and Samuel Jones, lying on the southeast of the last described one, I shall now take some notice of, having, since I commenced this letter, received some additional information concerning them. As noticed in a former letter, Woodford and Scott were quartered at these places. I have since understood that the residence of Samuel Jones was not at the place now occupied as Kendalt's tavern, on the State road; but the next farm above Samuel Richard's, in the Valley. The place, now Kendalt's, was, at the time of the encampment, occupied by a man named Anthony Moore, but who removed from the place shortly after, and before the close of the war, it was the residence of a person of the name of Samuel Jones, a relative of the former mentioned one. I have further learned that no officers were quartered, for any length of time, at Anthony Moore's.

Before proceeding to a further description of them, I will mention that I yesterday called on an old friend and relation, the venerable Lewis Walker of the city of Philadelphia, now near eighty-five years of age, whom I had not seen for near twenty years, and found him in possession of his mental and bodily powers, and actively engaged in his mercantile business. It was at his father's that Gen. Wayne was quartered, and he was at that time, more than ten years of age. From him I obtained the foregoing information, in addition to much other, which I shall insert in future numbers.

The farm, or rather farms, of Samuel Jones, for there were two of them—the one of them occupied by him at the time, the other by Jacob Fricke—are situated in the Great Valley. I do not know at what time he died. He left two sons, Enoch and Nathaniel, to whom the property descended. The farm of Enoch Jones, the place where Scott was quartered, has, since his death, been sold, and none of his descendants are now in possession of any part of it. The other one, I think, is still all held by descendants of Nathaniel Jones. In my conversation with Lewis Walker, he also informed me that, in addition to the general officers quartered at the different places, that in most instances, the field officers attached to the divisions and brigades, were mostly with them in their quarters. I shall give a full account of the staff attached to Gen. Wayne's brigade, in my next, as I received it from Lewis Walker.

The farm of Samuel Richards has, since his death, passed into several different hands. It was a highly productive farm, and still remains so. Samuel Richards died either during or soon after the Revolution. The property was held by some of his children and descendants, until the year 1815; since then it has been successively owned by Samuel Barry and Jonathan Phillips. It now belongs to some of the descendants of Jonathan Phillips. It has recently undergone many improvements in buildings and cultivation of soil.

In my next I shall have some occasion to make some addition to some former accounts, having received the information in the manner just related, and as they contain reminscences of the period of the encampment at Valley Forge, I hope that the introduction of them at this period of my narration, will not be looked upon as too great a digression in the order of time and place, in their arrangement.

Quarters of Gen. Scott

but better know as the quarters of Lord Howe, Commander of the British Army, original house, owned by Samuel Jones, now by Mr. Bodine, who has greatly remodeled it. See pages 58, and 113-4.

Quarters of Gen. Woodford

but previously the quarters of the Hessian General Kniphausen, the two parts to the right constituting the original house, the third part built in 1792 and the large part shortly before 1850, then owned by Samuel Richard, years ago known as the Dewees farm, now owned by A. G. McCollum. See pages 33, and 113-114.

Quarters of Gen. Lord Sterling

original house, owned by Rev. Wm. Currie, later by Jos. R. Walker, later by Sanderson, furnisher of the State Capitol, now greatly neglected, west of Valley Creek and west of residence of Sen. Knox. See p. 115.

Quarters of Gen. Pulaski

and for a time of Gen. Por, original building, owned by John Beaver, now by Frank Graham Thomson, who has called back the colonial home into the midst of modern culture. Here Devault Beaver shot the soldier for milking the cow. See pages 115 and 116, also 58 and 71.

LETTER XXV

FARM OF JOHN BEAVER

HE FARM of John Beaver was situated on the northeast of the farms of John Havard and John Brown. As noticed in my former letter, John Brown died about the time of the army encamping at the place; some officers were quartered for a short time at the place, but none permanently. Generals Poor and Pulaski, I have understood, were among the number. The latter was not stationary here. During the time he was connected with the cavalry, and they were mostly in the neighborhood of Trenton, in New Jersey. This property has been owned by Rev. William Currie, one of the King's chaplains, previously to the Revolution; but who, upon the war of the Revolution, was deprived of the privilege of officiating in that capacity, on account of his adherence to the royal cause. After disposing of this estate, he purchased another lying on the west side of the Valley Creek adjoining the Valley Forge estate, where he resided the remainder of his days. He lived to a very great age, and died since my recollection, I think in the year 1803, some of his descendants still occupying the property. It now belongs to Joseph R. Walker, his great grandson, and his mother, now near eighty years of age, resides with him. Levi Walker also informed me that General Stirling, a part of the time of the encampment, was quartered at this place; and that General Lee, the latter part of the time, was quartered at the house of David Havard, on the farm adjoining it on the southeast. Many of the descendants of Rev. William Currie still reside in that and other parts of the country and in the city of Philadelphia.

But to return to the farm of John Beaver. The most of it fell into the possession of his son, Devault Beaver, who, possessing the thrift, industry and economy, so peculiar to that useful and highly respectable portion of the inhabitants of Pennsylvania, the German farmer, he not only improved the fertility of the soil, but erected large, good and substantial buildings upon it; and by making additions to the original estate at different times, it became, in his life time, celebrated as one of the largest and most productive, as well as highly improved, farms in that section of country, a position it still continues to hold. He continued to reside upon it, increasing in wealth and prosperity, until his death, in the fall of 1837, in the eighty-second year of his age, leaving many descendants. Some of his sons have since deceased; the survivors of them are now engaged in the honorable employment of practical farmers. The property is now owned by his son-in-law.

FARMS OF JOSEPH WALKER

The farms of Joseph Walker will next claim our attention. At that time they consisted of two farms. The original mansion occupied by him is still standing. This farm was on the southwest of the place; the one occupied by his son, Isaac Walker, on the northeast. The whole tract of land contained more than three hundred acres, and is still held by the family. Its present owners are Joseph Walker, son of Isaac Walker, and Richard C. Walker and William Walker, sons of Thomas Walker. Richard C. Walker occupies the original mansion; and on the southeastern extremity of it, he has erected a small village, where several branches of mechanical business are conducted. It was here that Wayne was quartered. At the place where Joseph Walker now resides, General Greene was quartered. The middle section of the farm, held by William Walker, is of more recent origin, the buildings having all been erected since my recollection. It may be noted as rather an uncommon occurrence, that this part of the property is now in the sixth generation of the family. The present proprietors are men of industry and enterprise; and, while they have steadily increased in wealth, they have also increased in the value of their respective lands, by suitable, useful and commodious buildings and other improvements.

ABOUT GENERAL WAYNE

I shall now turn back to the period of the encampment, in order to insert some of the incidents of that period, related to me by Lewis Walker, in my recent conversation with him on the subject. He informed me that the staff of General Wayne consisted of Colonel Thomas Robinson, of Naaman's Creek, near the Pennsylvania and Delaware state line, Major Benjamin Fishbourne, of the city of Philadelphia, and Major Ryan of Virginia. These had their quarters in company with the General at his father's. I think I have heard it said that they were all connected with him either by relationship or marriage ties. In addition to these, there was also at their house, during the time, Dr. Robert Blackwell, of the city of Philadelphia, at that time a physician to the army, afterwards a clergyman, and for many years one of the officiating ministers of the united churches of Christ, St. Peters and St. James, in the city of Philadelphia, celebrated in his latter days for his immense wealth. Colonel Robinson spent the latter part of his life at his farm, on Naaman's Creek; and Major Fishbourne was first Governor of the North-Western Territory, then embracing all that section of country lying west of the Ohio river, and now divided into so many different states and territories, and teeming with inhabitants; and Major Ryan, after the war, returned to Virginia.

At the time they were quartered here, Wayne and Fishbourne each had in their service an Irishman in the capacity of waiters and to take care of their horses. The name of Wayne's servant was Patrick Joyce; and that of Fishbourne's was Philip—his other name could not be recalled. These two men undertook to rob them of their horses, clothing, money and other articles of value, they could get hold of, and then desert to the British. It so happened that the night fixed upon for carrying their design into execution, Colonel Robinson had occasion to rise early to attend to some duties, and not finding his change of raiment that had been brought home the preceding evening by his washer-woman, and placed by him in a situation that he knew where to find them, he proceeded to make a further search, and soon found that many other things had disappeared, among others the saddles and bridles of Wayne and Fishbourne, and their boots and pistols. He then alarmed the others, and the servants were observed in the act of taking the horses from the stable. The guard was ordered to stop them, which they did. In the morning they were tried, and each one sentenced to receive two hundred lashes on the bare skin. The sentence was carried into execution, Lewis Walker having been a witness to it. They were afterwards turned away, and, in all probability, went to the British.

During the time of the war, Joseph Walker endeavored as much as possible to take no part with either of the contending powers, he being a man of pacific principles, and a member of the Society of Friends. This gave occasion for many to condemn him as a Tory, by many of the Republican party, but such was his steady and consistent conduct through that trying and severe campaign, that he escaped with less loss of his property than many others. He had a large field of rye, and one of wheat, and the whole of his mowing ground, that was not destroyed, Wayne having placed a strong guard over them, to prevent the enclosures being taken away, or any person entering upon them. It was remarked in some of my former communications that the soldiers had suffered much from the small-pox; and this suffering was prolonged from being deprived of suitable food to facilitate their recovery. Lewis Walker, in our recent conversation, informed me that he well remembers them, in the spring of 1778, coming to their houses, bearing the marks of suffering, and craving of their benevolent mother, something to relieve their sufferings. One thing they particularly desired was vegetable food, as they had long been confined to the salted provisions of the camp. Their meadow abounded at that time with docks and other greens, but the guard would not permit them to enter. Upon making their complaints to her, she took the responsibility upon herself, told the guards to let them enter and collect them to boil with their salted provisions. They did so, and recovered gradually upon change of diet. Neither the guard, soldiers or herself were ever molested for the liberty they had taken.

A short time previous to the close of the campaign, he said a dinner party was given at his father's, by Gen. Wayne and staff, to the officers and many of their neighbors. A large temporary table, capable of accommodating a hundred persons was prepared for the occasion, under the shade of some trees near the house, where they partook of the dinner, there being more than a hundred persons who dined there on the occasion, the fare not being quite so sumptuous as some of our modern entertainment. Among the guests on the occasion was the Commander-in-Chief and his wife, the wife of General Wayne, and nearly all the generals and field officers of the encampment, and some of the neighbors of both sexes. He (Lewis Walker) says that he was sent to invite some of the officers on the occasion, and remembered the figure he made at the time. He mounted an old horse, without a saddle, with a blind halter instead of a bridle and thus equipped he rode barefooted about, to spread the invitations to them. He related to me many other things that occurred at the time, some of which have been noticed, others I shall omit.

Joseph Walker died in the year 1818, in the eighty-eighth year of his age, leaving a numerous family of descendants. Among the survivors of them are two of his sons—Lewis, from whom the most of the contents of this letter have been obtained; and Enoch Walker, now advanced in years and residing in Susquehanna county. His son, Isaac Walker, with whom Greene was quartered, resided at the same place all his days, and died in 1822 in the sixty-eighth year of his age, leaving also a numerous family of children and grandchildren, many of whom still reside in the neighborhood of the place.

I shall now conclude by requesting the publishers to forward to Lewis Walker, Market Street, between Eleventh and Twelfth, Philadelphia, and Enoch Walker, Dimmick Post Office, Susquehanna county, Pa., each a copy of the paper containing this number. In my next, I shall proceed with my description of the other properties where officers were quartered.

Quarters of Gen. Wayne

original house, owned by Joseph Walker, on a corner of his farm is located New Centerville. See pages 58 and 116-118.

Quarters of General Greene

"Rehobeth," the original home of the Walkers in the "Great Valley," on which is built the Friends' Meeting-house, parts of original wall still standing, owned by Isaac Walker, in 1850 by Jos. Walker, now by Charles Walker. See pages 58 and 116.

Quarters of Gen. Potter

erroneously accepted as the quarters of Gen. Mifflin, original house, bullet hole in the door, owned by Benj. Jones and occupied by Jacob Walker, birthplace of the authoress of the History of the Walker Family, now known as the "Little White Cottage," the quarters of Miss Anne Thomson's convalescent children. See pages 58 and 119 and Preface to Third Edition.

Quarters of Gen. Poor

original house part of present one, owned and occupied by Benj. Jones, now by Nathan Walker. See pages 58 and 119.

LETTER XXVI

THE FARM OF BENJAMIN JONES

THE FARMS where Potter, Poor, Mifflin and Sullivan were quartered, will next claim our attention. The farm of Jacob Walker had been disposed of at the time to Benjamin Jones. A part of it extended to the Front Line Hill, and in common with others, in similar situations, it was laid waste and the timber upon it destroyed, and some huts erected upon it. There were upon this farm two dwelling houses—Jacob Walker then occupying one; and Benjamin Jones, the other. The latter having purchased the whole of the property, he for several years carried on an extensive business in the manufactory of scythes and sickles, but had discontinued it before my recollection. He continued to reside on the farm the remainder of his days, and died at an advanced age, in the year 1815. The house in which he resided, and, where Poor was quartered, with a few acres of land, I think is still held by some of the family. The residue of the estate (the original mansion of Jacob Walker) is now owned by a person from Sheffield, in England, named Geo. Greaves, formerly extensively engaged in Sheffield, in the manufactory of various articles of cutlery and hardware. He does not at present reside on the property. This farm has been rented for many years, and though a highly productive one, yet it has not been improved as regards its buildings and appurtenances, as much as some of the others immediately surrounding it.

FARMS OF THOMAS WATERS

The farms of Thomas Waters adjoined this estate on the northeast. He owned a large body of land, consisting of four farms—three of them in the county of Chester, the other in the county of Montgomery. I shall now notice the two immediately adjoining the farm of Benjamin Jones. The others were not, as I have ever been informed remarkable for anything of sufficient importance, during the Revolution, to claim attention. One of the farms, at the time of the encampment, was occupied by William Godfrey. At this place Mifflin was quartered. He did not remain there during the whole time. He retired to Reading for a part of the time, in order to recruit his health and strength. William Godfrey, soon after the close of the war, removed to York county, where he died about the year 1813, advanced in years.

After the burning of the Valley Forge, the family of Colonel Dewees removed to this place and continued there for several years. While residing here he again resumed the manufacturing of iron at Valley Forge, and also engaged in a similar business at Heidelberg, in the now county of Lebanon. He became embarrased in his affairs, and was sold out by the Sheriff, and the latter part of his days was spent in poverty and neglect of the world. Thomas Waters died about the year 1791, and by will bequeathed his property to his grandson, Thomas W. Dewees. He soon dissipated the property, and disposed of it to a person named John Miller, a stone cutter of the city of Philadelphia, and a native of Scotland. He being a man of wealth and enterprise, soon after erected a large and substantial barn, finished in the most complete manner, and the second one of the kind erected in that portion of country, where so many similar ones have since been erected. John Miller died in 1814. The property was soon after sold to Hananiah Walker for two hundred dollars per acre. It is now owned by his two sons, and divided into two farms. This farm is justly celebrated for its fertility of soil, and for having water in every enclosure upon it.

The farm on which Thomas Waters lived during the Revolution was situate on the northwest of the one last described, and lying near the lines of the encampment, but not extending to them. It was here the Hessians found the money, and it was here the British drove away the cattle, and took many other things. Here General Sullivan was quartered, and it was here that Thomas Waters and Colonel Dewes both died. It was also here that the family of Colonel Dewees, after his embarrassment and the death of Thomas Waters, retired to reside. The property being bequeathed to Waters Dewees, subject to a life right in it for his mother, amounting in substance to the whole of the income of the farm. Colonel Dewees, as noticed in a former communication, died in the year 1809.

THE WIDOW OF COL. DEWEES INDEMNIFIED

About seven years after his death, his widow and some of the heirs, finding the papers relative to the claim on government, for damages sustained by the burning of Valley Forge, again resumed their petition to that body, and after carrying it through two successive sessions, in the first being negatived, but in the second passed by both houses, and a compensation of seven thousand, five hundred dollars allowed them. During the time of its prosecution, I was engaged in the store of a son-in-law of the Colonel's, in the city of Philadelphia, and had to call upon Caleb North, William Jackson, George A. Baker, and several others of the surviving officers of the Revolution, to procure their signatures to the of his having witnessed the conflagration from an eminence on Mount Joy. On account of his knowledge of the country, he being a native of Chester county, his place of abode not being more than twelve miles from the place, he had been sent, as noticed, incognito, to watch the movements of the detachment of the British army that destroyed it. Upon presenting him with the papers, he read them with emotion, particularly the certificates of Washington, Wayne, Mifflin and other officers of the Revolution, drawing at the same time the lively recollection of what he had beheld, and the scenes he had passed through, and observed that it required something more of him than a mere signature. He accordingly prepared a certificate setting forth a statement of the facts, to accompany the documents, to the city of Washington.

The widow of Colonel Dewees continued to reside here until the spring of 1821. The property was then sold to Mordecai Davis. It has since passed into the ownership of his son, Joseph Davis, the present proprietor. The widow of Colonel Dewees died at Valley Forge, in the latter part of 1822, aged near eighty years. This farm is fertile and highly productive in its nature. Upon it was erected in the year 1799, the first large and commodious stone barn in that part of the country, it being ninety feet in length, and forty-five in width. This farm has long been celebrated on account of the number of cattle that are annually fed upon it by its present owner, and also of the numerous agricultural products that are raised upon it, particularly wheat, Indian corn and hay.

FARM OF ABIJAH STEPHENS

All the property lying between this farm and the Front Line Hill, in Chester county, belonged at the time of the encampment to Abijah Stephens (my grandfather). Much has already been said concerning it, in connection with the accounts of the Revolution. I shall say but little further on the subject. The natural fertility of the soil is the same as those already mentioned as lying in the rich Valley of Chester county, but owing to its proximity to the camp, and other causes that I have mentioned, it not only suffered more severely, and was placed in a situation more difficult to overcome the disadvantages under which it was placed. My grandfather was a self-taught surgeon and practitioner in the art of healing ulcers, abscesses of various kinds, setting of broken bones and dislocations, curing spasms, cuts and bruises, but never undertook to attend in cases of sickness of any kind. At this time the number of physicians was very limited, and he having an extensive practise, did not engage in the resuscitating of his farm with that energy that characterized some others. The improvements were more gradual. In his life time the land was fenced, the soil cultivated, but with the exception of a new house erected by him, where he lived the latter part of his life, he erected no other buildings upon it. His farm, at the close of the Revolution, consisted of about three hundred and fifty acres of land, about one hundred and thirty of which he disposed of in his life time. He died on the twenty-first day of the eleventh month (November), one thousand, eight hundred and two, aged seventy years and nine months. He was born the same day as General Washington. Through life he sustained the character of an affectionate husband and father, friend and honest man, his fame as a practitioner, in various instances, is still remembered, and the virtue of his celebrated adhesive, sticking plaster will long be remembered, and used as a valuable and important family acquisition.

He left at his death, one son and six daughters. By will he bequeathed the great body of his land to his son, Stephen Stephens, who deceased about five years ago. The original mansion and other buildings on the property, at the time of the Revolution, have all been superceded by new ones, and since his death that part of the estate has been divided into three parts, and it is now owned by one of his sons, who resides near the original mansion. His daughter owns another portion of it, and three of his grandchildren the residue. A part of this property is now in possession of the sixth generation of the lineal descent of Evan ap Bevan, their original ancestor.

A small portion, consisting of eleven acres of land, with the appurtenances, has recently, on account of the death of one of the daughters of Abijah Stephens, been disposed of out of the family. The residue is still in possession of some branches of the family. The descendants of Abijah Stephens are very numerous, though but few of them now bear the name.

I have now finished a description of all the property lying in the county of Chester, as contemplated in my original design. In my next I shall proceed to that portion lying in the county of Montgomery.

I had originally anticipated concluding these narratives with this number, but I find I shall not be able to do so, as there are yet some very interesting accounts of the improvements that have lately taken place, and some occurrences and reminiscences that have transpired in that section of country, particularly in that portion of it that has not yet been fully described. I shall, therefore, be under the necessity of adding a few more additional numbers to those that have been finished.

Quarters of Gen. Mifflin

original house razed, site designated by x, having stood across lane from the barn, present house some distance to northeast, owned by Thos. Waters, tenanted by Wm. Godfrey, within present recollection home of Havard Walker, now by Commissioner John R. K. Scott. See pages 58 and 119 and 120, also the Preface to Third Edition.

Quarters of Gen. Sullivan

original house razed, but foundation, about 50 feet in length, clearly discernible, to rear of the present house, home of Thos. Waters, long known as a Davis farm, now owned by Commissioner John R. K. Scott. See pages 38, 40-41, 58, 120-121.

Quarters of Gen. Morgan and the Commissary General

original building and cave, owned by Mordecai Moore, later by Alexander Kennedy, then by David Zook, now by Sen. Croft. See pages 57, 123-124.

Quarters of Gen. Muhlenberg

original house, east of Port Kennedy, owned by John Moore, now by Mr. Irvin. See pages 57, 124-125.

LETTER XXVII

THE MOORE PROPERTIES

HE PROPERTY embraced in the lines of the encampment, and lying in the northeastern and northern section of it, in the county of Montgomery, will claim our notice in this communication. The greater portion of this property at that time belonged to John and Mordecai Moore, and has been noticed in some former numbers. On this property fortifications were constructed and pickets placed. At John Moore's, which was the furthest from Headquarters, Muhlenberg was quartered in company with a number of inferior officers; and at the house of Mordecai Moore, the Commissary General of the army was stationed, and General Morgan was occasionally quartered at the place.

Much has been already said concerning this property in the general account of the encampment. I shall, therefore, in this number inform my readers, that Mordecai Moore continued to reside there till the spring of 1801. He had raised a family of six sons and two daughters; these had all left him previous to that time. His daughters were married, and his sons had principally removed to other parts of the country to seek their fortunes—some as mechanics and two as professional men. He and his wife, being advanced in years and the property resuscitated from the effects of the war, removed to Abington township in the same county, to reside with their son, who was settled there as a practitioner of medicine, and rented his farm during the residue of his life. He died at Abington in the summer of 1803, advanced in years.

ALEXANDER DENNEDY

Some time after his decease, the property was sold to Alexander Kennedy, a native of Ireland, who removed to reside upon it in 1805, and continued there until his death, in the fall of 1844, aged sixty-three years. From a small beginning upon his arrival in this country, he increased in wealth and property, and at the same time by an exemplary life and character, he lived universally respected, and died sincerely lamented, not only by his family, but also by a large circle of friends and acquaintances. I may here notice something concerning him, that shows the reverses of fortune that people sometimes pass through. When he first arrived in the country, he was engaged in the capacity of a footman, to a person in the neighborhood, of a haughty disposition, and it was his business to hold his horse, follow him on foot from place to place, to take care of it when he rode out in his chair, and perform other menial services. In the course of a few years time became altered; the servant became a man of wealth and respectability, the master became a poor, distressed and debilitated object, scarcely able to travel from one house to another—an evidence of the truth of the declaration of the wise man, that "pride goeth before destruction, and a haughty spirit before a fall." I have seen him when thus reduced, ask of Alexander Kennedy to allow him the privilege of riding in his ox-cart, such were the reverses of fortune that had overtaken him. But to resume the subject

After the decease of Alexander Kennedy, his family continued to reside on the property, until the spring of 1837. It was then sold to David Zook, the present owner and occupant of the greater part of it. He married a granddaughter of Mordecai Moore, so that a part of the property has now got into possession of a branch of its original owner. The southwestern portion of the farm, that part on which the huts and breastworks were erected, is now owned by Abraham Beidler. The whole of the property originally belonging to the Moore family, and owned by Alexander Kennedy at the time of his death, consisting of more than two hundred acres, is under a state of high cultivation and is abundantly productive, and continues improving under the present enterprising owners of it.

The farm or rather farms of John Moore will now claim our attention. As noticed in a former letter, John Moore, the owner of them, at the time Muhlenberg took up his headquarters at the place, died soon after, on the first day of the year 1778. Two of his sons, John and Richard Moore, took possession of the property. The mansion where Muhlenberg was quartered was taken by Richard Moore, and was the farthest extent of the lines of encampment in a northeastern direction, and nearest to the city of Philadelphia. Another farm, lying on the west of this property and nearer the Schuylkill, the one on which the fort was erected, and also a considerable number of the huts, was taken by John Moore. They both held these farms during their lives. John Moore died in the spring of 1822, and Richard Moore in the fall of 1823; they both were at their decease between sixty-five and seventy years of age. During their lifetimes they had each purchased considerable real estate adjoining their paternal farms, which will be noticed in some future numbers. The children of John Moore now own none of the real estate; it has passed into the ownership of different persons—some during his lifetime, the residue since his death. The two sons of Richard Moore, Edwin and Samuel, now own all the real estate of their father held by him at his decease; and the former one now (1850) owns the mansion and about seventy acres of the farm of John Moore. These farms, together with the others I have been describing, are all situated in the Great Valley; and for richness of soil, convenience of market, contiguity of railroads, canals and turnpikes, abundance of limestone and other advantages which might be enumerated, are such as place it in a situation that is not excelled by any other portion of country in Eastern Pennsylvania. On the farm of Edwin Moore are several large and beautiful springs of limestone water. They issue out of the northwest side of a hill about a mile from the Schuylkill, supplying in their course a large flouring mill with a constant supply of water; and so uniform is the quantity that it is not impeded by drought in summer or frost in winter. To describe the beauty of the largest of these springs and the transparency of the water issuing from them in a meandering course until it reaches the mill dam, is not in my power. They must be seen to be duly appreciated. The stream in my earlier days used to be noted for its abundance of fine trout, and was much frequented by anglers. To the truth of this assertion my friend, William Henry, of Doylestown, can bear ample proof. Of late they have much decreased. Belonging to Edwin and Samuel Moore is a piece of land containing, in connection with about fifteen acres of land in Montgomery county, now in possession of our family, that is known by the name of the mine land on account of its having been purchased about one hundred and fifty years ago (1700) by a company of people for the purpose of digging for copper. As the business of mining in this line has recently been commenced in many places in that vicinity, I shall devote a greater portion of time to a more general account of it in some future numbers.

The greater part of the country that I have described on the western side of the Schuylkill, particularly that part lying in the Great Valley, was laid waste, and but little exertion was made by most of the owners of it to improve it until after the conclusion of the war. They then commenced the restoration of their farms. The hand of industry soon caused the face of the country to assume a different aspect, but it was for many years after before some of it was restored. In commencing this work they encountered many difficulties. Continental money died on their hands. The government was for many years after in a very unsettled state. The foreign trade was crippled by the war. And many other discouraging circumstances had to be surmounted by persevering industry and patient resignation. In a few years these were overcome; their lands were enclosed; where lately nothing was beheld but desolation could be seen the fruitful fields crowned with abundance of grain of every description, for the sustenance of man and beast, and in summer clad with verdant grass, on which flocks and herds were quietly feeding and the whole face of the country bearing witness of the blessings of peace in contrast with the evils of war. The adoption of the present Constitution of the United States, the revival of trade and commerce, the demand of our produce in foreign ports, and the establishment of a sound currency, soon placed the agricultural interests of that period on a firm and lucrative foundation.

A DIGNIFIED VISITOR IN A PLAIN SUIT OF BLACK

I shall close this communication with an account I have often heard related by my father. In the latter part of the summer of 1796, he was engaged in ploughing in a field near the Front Line Hill. It was in the afternoon of the day, and he observed an elderly person of a very dignified appearance, dressed in a plain suit of black, on horseback, accompanied by a black waiter, ride to a place in the road opposite to him, where he alighted from his horse and came into the field to him, and shaking hands cordially with him, told him he had called to make some inquiry of him, concerning the owners and occupants of the different places about there, and also in regard to the system of farming practised in that part of the country, the kinds of grain and vegetables raised, the time of sowing and planting, the best method of tilling the ground, the quantity raised, and numerous other things relative to farming and agriculture, and asking after some families in the neighborhood. As answers were given he noted them down in a memorandum book.

My father informed him that he was unable to give as correct information as he could wish, as he had not been brought up to the farming business, and was not a native of that part of the country, having settled there since the war, that he came from North Carolina, where he resided previous to the Revolution, that he had been in the army and was one of the number encamped there during the war. This gave a new turn to the conversation. The stranger informed him that he had also been in the army and encamped there, and was expecting in a few months to leave the city of Philadelphia, with no prospect of ever returning. He had taken a journey to visit the place, view the old encampment ground, which had been the scene of so much suffering and distress, and see how far the inhabitants were recovering from the disasters they had experienced, and the losses they had sustained from that event, adding that his name was George Washington.

Upon receiving this information, my father told him that his costume and appearance were so altered that he did not recognize him, or he would have paid more respect to his old Commander and the Chief Magistrate of the Union. He replied that to see the people happy and satisfied, and the desolate fields recovering from the disasters they had experienced, and particularly to meet with any old companion of his in arms and suffering now peacefully engaged in the most useful of all employments, afforded him more real satisfaction than all the servile homage that could be paid to his person or station. He then asked his name, noted it in his memorandum book, and said that pressing engagements rendered it necessary for him to return to the city that night, or he would visit some of his former friends at their houses. Then taking him by the hand bade him an affectionate farewell.

In my next, I shall describe the property in the county of Montgomery, in the lines of the encampment, lying on the river.

LETTER XXVIII

LAETITIA PENN'S MANOR

HE PROPERTY I shall now proceed to describe consists of a tract of land lying in the county of Montgomery, on the river Schuylkill, extending down the same from the Valley Forge tract to the north of a small stream (originally called Cedar Creek), and bounded on the southeast by a line called the Bilton Line, commencing near the mouth of the stream, and running a southwesterly course until it strikes the Valley Creek, a part of said line being the county line of Chester and Montgomery counties.

This tract containing more than a thousand acres was called "Laetitia Penn's Manor," on account of it having been given by William Penn to his daughter Laetitia. The greater part of it has been referred to as the property of David Stephens, William Smith and the place where the commander of the Second Regiment was quartered.

THE JENKINS-MORRIS FARM

There is one farm lying on the river, adjoining the latter one, and still lower down, that having suffered in some measure from the effects of the encampment, I shall therefore take some notice of it. This was owned by a person named Jenkins. He first settled there more than one hundred years ago (before 1750). From him a pool in the river, celebrated for its depth and good fishing, and also an island took their names.

This property passed into other hands, more than eighty years ago. But whether sold by him in his life time or since his death, I cannot say. He died about that time. My mother deceased a little more than three years since, in the eighty-ninth year of her age, remembered him, though she was very young at the time of his death. He was a Welshman, and used to converse with her grandmother in that language. This was the principal recollection she had of him. At the time of the Revolution and for more than twenty years after, it belonged to Robert Morris, the great financier and the founder of Morrisville in this county (Bucks). After his embarrassment it was sold by the Sheriff to John Moore, and, with the exception of the mill and appurtenances and fifteen acres of land sold to Isaac Beaver, it was held by him till his death in 1822. It was soon after sold to Dennis Conard, the present owner and occupant. The original mansion erected by Jenkins is, I think, still standing on the property, though new and substantial buildings have been erected upon it by the present proprietor. At the time of the war this property was occupied by a minister of the Society of Friends, named Abraham Griffith, and it is more than probable that some officers may have been quartered there. It suffered some little destruction of timber from the soldiers, but owing to its distance from the main body of the encampment, it was not so much devastated as some others.

While this property belonged to Robert Morris, he used sometimes to form parties for the purpose of fishing for the speckled trout that abounded in the stream on and near the premises, to which he invited the President and heads of the different departments of government, members of Congress and other distinguished officers and citizens of Philadelphia, numbers of whom often attended on these occasions for the two-fold object of enjoying the pleasure of the party and visiting the old ground of the encampment.

PORT KENNEDY

The farm mentioned as the quarters of the commander of the Second Regiment, and the next in course as we proceed up the river, with the next one above, where the provost's guard was placed, were originally owned by a person named Eglington, who left two daughters, to whom the property descended. One of them named Mary, to whom the former one belonged, married a person named David Riley, and for some years resided upon it. This was previous to the Revolution. They mortgaged this property to a person named Thomas Hazelton, and neither principal or interest of the mortgage was paid. The Rileys moved off the property, and upon the death of Hazelton, the claim descended to his two daughters, who took possession of it by virtue of the mortgage. One of them married a sea captain named Alexander Hodgson, the other went to England, lived there the remainder of her days, and died unmarried within the last thirty years. Alexander Hodgson died more than forty years ago. His widow died since my removal to this county (about 1828). They left no children.

My first recollection of this property was when in the fourth year of my age. It was then occupied by Michael Shur. It was then called Hodgson's place, and celebrated on account of a great spring that rises upon it by two distinct heads, which issue from under a large beech tree, and unite together immediately after flowing from the hill. Either of these springs are as large as Ingham's great spring in this county, but rising so near the river, and not possessing sufficient natural advantages, the water power has never been used for manufacturing purposes. There is one thing remarkable about these springs, that is, that though they rise within a few feet of each other, the one is soft sandstone, the other hard limestone water.

This place having with others suffered from the effects of the encampment, it did not, like some others, advance in the same course of improvement. The greater part of it lay a common for more than fifty years after, doubts as to the ownership of it preventing much improvement being made upon it. The Hazelton family holding it by virtue of the mortgage, and the Riley family having moved off without paying principal or interest, or in any other way disposing of it, the fences went to decay. The buildings were poor and trifling, the soil became exhausted, and for many years previous to the year 1820, the greater part of it was the picture of desolation and barrenness.

About this time seven-sixteenths of the whole estate was sold by an agent of the widow Hodgson to Alexander Kennedy, John Elliott, John Frick and Lewis Wanwag. The other sixteenth which was her full share, was retained by the agent until a disputed line should be settled. Previous to the fall of 1824, Alexander Kennedy purchased all the right and interest in the property belonging to John Elliott and Lewis Wanwag, so that at the time of his decease he was owner of three-eighths of the whole estate. Since that time his heirs have purchased the right and title of all the other owners, thus becoming absolute owners of the whole property. The estate, with the exception of some building lots, and about thirteen acres of limestone land, the latter sold to Robert Bethel, formerly of this county, now belongs to William, David R., and John Kennedy. There is now (1850) on this property more than fifty houses, sixty lime kilns in constant operation, employing more than four hundred men; a large hotel, three stories high and forty feet square; four stores, two blacksmith shops and wheelwright shops; and numerous other manufacturing trades carried on at the place; and two lumber yards and several coal yards, doing an extensive business.

This place is called Port Kennedy, and is celebrated for the great quantity of lime that is burnt, and shipped in canal boats annually from there to various parts of the states of Pennsylvania, New Jersey, Delaware and Maryland. The amount sent from this place during last year, I was informed by two of the proprietors, was more than one million, two hundred and fifty thousand bushels. We may then safely hazard the opinion that it is the most extensive operation, in that line of business, in the Union. Here, at times and seasons, on working days, if some unavoidable circumstance does not prevent, may be seen the jolly sons of Emerald Isle, some driving their carts loaded with lime and coal, to and from the river, some hauling stones to fill the kilns, others are quarrying, some engaged in filling, while others are loading carts, and, in fact all the different operations attendant upon it, are conducted at the same time, at different kilns, belonging to the same person. Each of the workmen appearing to enjoy themselves in their different avocations, if the joyous song or merry whistle may be taken as an evidence of contentment. The boats that carry the lime from the place are large and commodious, and of late the most of them furnished with masts and sails to be used in tide-water. They generally contain about three thousand bushels.

In addition to the different branches of business mentioned above, it may also be noticed that the arable land has been much improved by the present active and enterprising owners; so that the land which for half a century lay barren and unproductive, a waste and almost useless common, now abounds with plenty, and is enclosed, producing an abundance of the fruits of the earth for the sustenance of mankind. An evidence of the truth of it is apparent by the large and well-filled barns on the premises.

The Reading Railroad passes through the property, and last year (1849) a bridge was constructed across the river, which more intimately connects the business on both sides of the river; and while it is of mutual benefit, it will have a tendency to still enhance the value of real estate in the immediate vicinity; though it is now to be regretted that recent injuries done to it by freshets have rendered it at present unfit for crossing with vehicles of any kind. It is now being repaired.

The quarries and limekilns on this property are objects of great importance, but I shall fail giving a full description of them. These, independent of other things, equally interesting, would be worthy of a visit. The limestone lies near the surface, and is easily quarried. There are two hills of considerable elevation extending about three-fourths of the whole length of the farm, which are a solid body of limestone. A small vale of about sixty feet in width passes between them, and gradually descends toward the river, which is the great thoroughfare for the numerous teams employed in conducting the business. Acres of ground have been excavated for the purpose of procuring limestone. In some places roads or cartways have been cut through solid bodies of limestone and lead to quarries belonging to different persons, one of which I lately examined. It had then a base line on a level with the causeway, of about one hundred and thirteen feet. Its perpendicular height was obout eighty feet, and it extended in length more than two hundred feet. This quarry is owned by David Zook, who has purchased a small portion of the estate, and is extensively engaged in the lime business. A public road now passes through this property, between these two hills, and leads from Port Kennedy, through a part of the old encampment, to the Gulf Road. The lime kilns are erected at various places—

some on the river, others on both sides of the road just mentioned, generally from six to twelve abreast, and containing from two to three thousand bushels. It may also be observed that several large basins have been excavated on the river, for the purpose of boats entering to receive and discharge their cargoes, and there are also a few docks for boats to enter for similar purposes.

The greater part of the business of the place is done through the medium of the canal. Coal and lumber are brought in this way—the former from the mines in the county of Schuylkill, the latter generally from the Susquehanna by way of the Union Canal. Little business is done here, or at any other place on the river by the Reading Railroad, when the navigation is open, except that the mail is transported by the locomotive train of cars, and a passenger train stops daily at this place. There is a postoffice also established here, called Port Kennedy Postoffice. The Reading Railroad is chiefly employed in conveying coal from Pottsville to Richmond on the Delaware, having enough to do in that line. Much more might be said concerning the changes and improvements this property has undergone within the last twenty years, were it deemed requisite. Enough has been said to show the blessings of peace, enterprise and industry, in contrast with the curses of war, devastation and destruction.

I shall conclude with some observations that I heard made a few years ago by an old man now living in Abington township, Montgomery county, who resided at Port Kennedy forty-six years ago.

He was returning from Pottsville in a boat, which stopped for a short time at the place, and he availed himself of the opportunity of taking a view of the property, but everything was strange around him. He went to view the spring, the old house in which he lived, the waste fields and other objects which he left there. The spring still remained, but the site of it, in its native beauty, had been destroyed by buildings erected over it. Instead of the old house and miserable barn, new and splendid buildings had been erected upon it; the waste fields were enclosed, and the whole face of it had undergone a thorough change, and the only objects that he could see to remind him of the days of his residence there were an old shellbark hickory tree (a part of which is still remaining) (1850), and the large limestone rock on the bank of the river. There, he said, were all he could recognize, and in narrating the account he observed that if he could have been placed there, without previous knowledge of his locality, he could not possibly have known where he was, so great had been the change. In relating this account I was forcibly reminded of Washington

Irving's humorous tale of Rip Van Winkle sleeping twenty years on the Catskill Mountain, and awakening and finding himself a stranger to everything transpiring around him.

LETTER XXIX

THE PROVOST FARM

N THIS communication I shall first proceed to give a description of the farm on which the provost guard was placed during the Revolution, and the officers having charge of it were quartered. At the time the property containing one hundred and twenty-five acres was owned by William Smith, first President of the University of Pennsylvania, and then occupied by a person, as a tenant, named Henry Force. The provost was kept in an old log barn on the premises, that stood as a relic of that period until 1830; it was then demolished and a new and commodious stone barn erected near the site of the old one. This place having within the last twenty years undergone much alteration, it will, therefore, claim considerable attention. In order that the account may be kept in a connected form, I shall now refer to the early hitsory of the place. As observed in my last, this property was originally owned by a person named Eglington, and at his death, it fell to his daughter, who sold it to Henry Pawling, the grandfather of Levi Pawling, mentioned in one of my former letters. While in his possession he added to it an island in the river, called Catfish island (noted on account of a large buttonwood tree growing on it at the time, cut down thirty years since), he taking up and patenting another called Fatland Island, about a half mile higher up the river. It has since that time had many owners, numbers of them I shall not refer to, as they cannot particularly interest many readers. I shall, therefore, just observe that from the time of the Proprietor of Pennsylvania granting it to his daughter, up to the year 1812, it had passed through sixteen different conveyances. I have never heard anything more of sufficient notice occurring here during the time of the encampment to claim any further observation. It suffered in common with others contiguous to it. I shall, therefore, pass by that period, and confine myself to incidents that have occurred since my recollection, which extends back to the commencement of the present century. It was then I first remember being upon it. I was then in the fifth year of my age; it was at that time owned by Andrew Porter, the father of David E. Porter, Ex-Governor of Pennsylvania, and in the

occupancy of Michael Shur. As noted, it had suffered from the effects of the war, and having changed owners and tenants so often it had not improved much either in quality or appearance at that period. It was soon after sold to a person named Stephen Kingston from Philadelphia, who held it about four years.

During the time the property was owned by Stephen Kingston, he made considerable alterations upon it, and transformed the appearance of part of it, but made very little useful or durable improvements; although enough was expended upon it, in enclosing three sides of a ten acre with a stone wall of solid masonry, four and a half feet high and eighteen inches thick, and erecting an ungainly stone edifice covering much ground and affording little room to have erected suitable buildings of all kinds necessary for the accommodation of such a farm. There was also expended by him in making pleasure gardens and fish ponds, and endeavoring to rear tropical fruit and numerous other things equally useless, to have closed the whole estate with good and substantial fence. How much further he would have extended these things is uncertain, his avowed object being (as it might seem) to effect these things first, and then improve the land. But the means failed; he became embarrassed, the place was sold, and then the work ceased to be carried on. They gradually fell into decay; and at this time there is scarcely anything except the house, which has undergone some alterations, left on the premises, to remind the observer of the existence of these things.

Its next owner was George Davis, from the city of Philadelphia; he held it about two years. It subsequently fell into possession and ownership of Frederick Weisel. It was disposed of to Samuel Richards in the year 1811, who continued to reside in it until the year 1824. It was then sold to Thomas J. Walker, who removed to reside upon it in the spring of that year. While held by Samuel Richards, he sold off the southeastern part of it, about thirty-two acres, which reduced it down to about ninety-three acres.

During the time it was held by the persons last mentioned, no improvement of any consequence was made upon it. The land grew but little if any better in quality, many of the enclosures had gone to decay, and that part that was sold by Samuel Richards was turned out as a useless common, and had remained so for a number of years.

The death of Thomas J. Walker occurred about five months after his removal to the place. He was an enterprising man, and had his life been spared a few years longer, he would no doubt have improved the property. It was held by his executors until the spring of 1828, when it was disposed of by them to Isaac Sharpless, who at that time took up his residence upon it. The

The History of Valley Forge 135

most of the soil was good, and all it wanted was proper cultivation.

The period had now arrived when this place was to assume a different appearance, under management of its then thrifty, industrious and enterprising owner. Independent of its natural good soil, it possessed other advantages; it abounded in limestone of a superior quality. The navigation of the Schuylkill had been fully completed; the spirit of improving the soil by the application of lime as a manure, or rather fertilizer of the soil, was now engaging the attention of farmers in various sections of the country, particularly those to whom the navigation of the river opened an easy facility of obtaining it through that medium. Hence extensive trade in that line was opened, not only to various parts of our own state, both up and down the river, but also in various parts of the states of New Jersey, Delaware and Maryland. These combined advantages being improved by the owner of the property, it soon began to assume a very different appearance.

The useless stone wall was taken down, and the materials used for constructing a large stone barn, and other convenient and necessary buildings. The fences were all renewed by good and substantial ones; and the place seen at the time he took possession of it as the scene of dilapidation and decay, now wears a bright prospect—a monument of the enterprise of its last industrious owner.

While owned by Isaac Sharpless, he disposed of all that portion of it lying on the southeast side of a public road leading from Port Kennedy to the Valley Forge, except a small portion reserved for limestone. On this part of the farm, an extensive business in the manufacturing of lime is carried on principally by Richard C. Walker and sons, but not to so great an extent as at Port Kennedy—the business at this place conducted by them being more generally to parts of Montgomery, Chester and Delaware counties, and hauled by large teams, though considerable is done by canal and railroad. On this portion of the property several good dwellings have been erected since it came into their possession, together with a dwelling house, wheelwright and blacksmith shop, erected by others, there being about one hundred inhabitants residing upon it.

The Reading Railroad passes through this farm, between the original mansion and the river; and from the house can be enjoyed an uninterrupted view of both the railroad and the river. Here at all hours of the day, may be seen and heard the numerous trains of coal and other cars, continually ascending and descending upon the railroad, conveying daily thousands of tons of anthracite coal, from the extensive mines in Schuylkill county, to Richmond on the Delaware, in the city of Philadelphia, and other productions of the soil, and articles of manufacture and merchandise. In addition to these, when the navigation is unobstructed may be seen large coal boats, passing to and from the same regions; and others laden with lumber and other articles, by way of the Union Canal, from various parts of the interior of our own state. I have often seen more than a dozen large boats of this description at one view from the place, thus engaged.

It may be also noticed that a lumber and coal yard was commenced on this property by Dr. Jones Davis, about the year 1832; but it has for several years been abandoned. I have now in this and my last letter, given a general account of these two estates, that lay waste so many years, and have recently undergone so much improvement. In doing so I have had considerable allusion to the business done on the Reading Railroad and the Schuylkill Canal, and I hope I will be excused, if I through this medium, just suggest to the people of Bucks county, particularly those in the vicinity of New Hope, Doylestown, and other places immediately on the route, the advantages that would accrue to them if a railroad from New Hope to Norristown could be constructed. I merely mention them; at present I shall make no further comments on them; but resume my general subject.

THE DAVID STEPHENS FARMS

The property belonging to David Stephens is now the only one that remains to be described that was embraced in the lines of the encampment. It consisted of two farms, extending from the last described one unto the Valley Forge tract, and lying upon the river Schuylkill.

The lower one, at the time of the war, was occupied by a person named Zachary Davis; and at his house General Huntingdon had his quarters. This farm, which was large and valuable, after the death of David Stephens, which I think was about the year 1786, fell to his son, Maurice Stephens, more generally known by the name of Esquire Stephens, on account of his holding the commission of a justice of the peace for more than thirty-five years. He lived and died unmarried, and not being very energetic, he did not improve his farm to any great extent, except that he erected a large and commodious barn and house upon it. He became involved, and spent the great part of it during his life time; he died in the fall of 1827. For some years before his death he was blind, and his faculties were impaired.

The property, about two years previous to his death, was sold to William Henry, of the county of Philadelphia, who now resides upon it, having removed there shortly after purchasing it. The property has been much improved since it has come into his possession; part of it that had laid a common since the Revolution, and probably longer, has been enclosed, and now is under a high state of cultivation; additional buildings have been erected upon it, and other land lying contiguous to it has been purchased by him, so that it now stands conspicuous as one of the largest and most highly cultivated farms in that portion of the ground of the encampment. William Henry is at present one of the representatives in the legislature of Pennsylvania.

On this property there was a number of huts erected, though I do not know of any fortifications or breastworks being thrown up on it. It was in a hut on this property, that Baron Steuben resided during a part of the time of the encampment, being engaged in teaching the soldiers military tactics; and it was upon it that the soldiery were exercised by him on these occasions. I have heard my father relate the awkward blunders and confusion that often occurred at such times, on account of the Baron being unable to speak the English language, and the soldiers not understanding his orders and instructions given in German.

The next farm above was where David Stephens resided. Varnum was quartered upon this part of the farm; and near the mansion the fort was erected that I have noticed in a former number, upon an eminence commanding a view of both sides of the river. There are very few traces of it left remaining; but its site can be pointed out by many persons, as well as myself, who remember to have seen it before it was destroyed. A beautiful prospect of the surrounding country can be enjoyed by this eminence. This part of the property since his death was owned by his son, Abijah Stephens. He made during his life time many improvements upon it, by the addition of suitable and commodious buildings, and also in the improvement of the soil. The mansion in which Vernum dwelt is standing. Abijah Stephens died in the fall of 1825, aged sixty-seven years. The property is now owned by his son, William Stephens, who resides upon it.

The residue of the farm of David Stephens, consisting of more than one hundred and twenty acres, fell into possession of his only daughter, Eleanor Richardson; she died about 1820. The most of it now belongs to her children, though some of it had passed into other hands in her life time, and some since her death. On part of this property many of the remains of the encampment still (1850) remain visible, such as fortifications, breastworks (particularly the fort used for the magazine), and the traces of the foundations of the huts. It was opposite the upper end of this property, on the river, that Sullivan's bridge was erected; next above it on the river, were the Headquarters of General Washington.

I have now finished the description of all the property embraced in the lines of the encampment; and a few more communications will finish this prolonged account.

LETTER XXX

MINERALS

HE DISCOVERY of large quantities of copper on some of the property I have been describing, and, also upon lands lying contiguous to the Valley Forge and Pickering, a stream that empties into the Schuylkill about three miles above Valley Forge, having recently attracted much attention, and enhanced the value of property, particularly that portion of it last noticed. I shall proceed in this communication to give some account concerning it.

In some former letters, I observed, concerning that portion of country, that recent discoveries and establishment of some manufactories on a small scale, had made some innovations upon the regular habits of the inhabitants resident upon it. Since the geological survey of Pennsylvania, discoveries have been made of the existence of copper in its natural state, in many places in the vicinity of Valley Forge, and the attention of capitalists has recently been turned towards mining operations in that line. For this purpose two companies have been organized, and large tracts or portions of land lying on both sides of the Schuylkill, in the counties of Chester and Montgomery, have been secured by them, either by purchase or lease for a number of years, in order to carry on the business. The land supposed to contain the article, lying between the Valley Forge and Pickering Creek, have been purchased by a company from Philadelphia, called Remington & Co. The other company, I have understood, are Englishmen from Cornwall in England, called Pedrick & Co., and that they have leased portions of land in Montgomery county, on both sides of the river, and that the operations are now being carried on by them with every prospect of success.

I shall now refer to some remarks, in a recent communication, concerning a tract of land, a part of which is now owned by Edwin or Samuel Moore, that was purchased for a similar purpose near one hundred and fifty years ago. Copper, at that time, was known to exist on that land, and it was then purchased by a company, and operations in that line commenced, not so much for the sake of the copper as the hope that they would also find, in connection with it, silver and gold in abundance. For this purpose numerous pits were dug in various places upon the northeastern part of it; and I have understood that enough of copper was obtained for the purpose of defraying the expenses of digging, and to enable the company to pay for the land. But at that early period the people had not the advantages which we now possess; mechanic arts had made but little progress, and for want of the means of pumping the water by hydraulic apparatus, they had, in all cases, after sinking the pit to nearly a uniform depth, encountered springs of water so abundant as to arrest their progress and put an end to their labors. In process of time, all further efforts to obtain not only gold and silver, but even copper, were entirely abandoned, and the land lay uncultivated and unimproved for many years, until it fell into possession of my grandfather and Thomas Waters. A part of it held by my grandfather is still in possession of a part of the family. The residue, since his death, and that portion owned by Thomas Waters, has all of it passed, within the last fifty years, into the ownership of Richard Moore, the father of the present owners of it. I may just observe that while a part of this property was owned by the late Stephen Stephens, a quarry of gypsum was supposed to be discovered upon it; but if so, it has never amounted to anything further than a supposed discovery. A portion of this tract was taken by Pedrick & Co., for the purpose of mining for copper. I may here observe that about the time the mining was in operation, about the commencement of the last century, that similar operations were commenced on the property of my great-grandfather, Stephen Evans, and that the remains of numerous pits are still visible, lying on the Gulf road, on the farm of the late Stephen Stephens, in Chester county. Tradition says, that copper was found there to some extent, but the same cause that frustrated their design on the mine tract, operated against them at that place, and the work was abandoned. I have no doubt that copper does exist in that particular section, from the fact that in digging wells about the depth of thirty feet, water is generally obtained, and it has been found in some instances, to taste strongly of copper, and when taken up in a tin or earthen vessel and left to stand for some time, a thick sediment, resembling a solution of copperas, is found settled in the bottom of the vessel.

Another peculiarity of this tract that I have been describing, is the kind of stone found on and near its surface. It is of that kind commonly called the honey-comb, on account of its light porous nature and its supposed resemblance to the honey-comb of the bee. It abounds on what is called the mine tract, generally lying on the surface or in detached rocks fast in the ground, many of them crystallized, with crystals of various sizes, the most of them of a clear white color, with four regular sides, and terminating in a point so sharp and hard that glass has sometimes been cut with them. Many of these crystals lie loose on the ground, but the great body of them are found adhering to the honey-comb stone. Many buildings have been erected in the neighborhood with this kind of stone; they are very light, and on this account, they are very useful, as they do not require much bodily strength to raise them to the top of the building. Although very light and porous, yet they form a solid substantial wall and are impervious to water. Many other varieties of minerals are found in that district; so much so that they have attracted the attention of mineralogists, and numerous specimens of them have been obtained to place in cabinets of different persons. I have collected many of them and forwarded them to different persons. Some of them I think may be found in the extensive mineral cabinet of my friend, John Watson, of Greenville, Buckingham township, Bucks county.

I have never heard of any iron being found in any part of the country immediately in the vicinity of Valley Forge; and from the circumstance that very little attraction of the needle has ever been noticed on any part of the property that I have described (except in the immediate locality of the old Valley Forge and other iron works), and no furnaces ever having been erected there, I conclude that it does not exist in that section. It has recently been found in abundance in the neighborhood of Kimberton, in Pikeland township, in Vincent and other places in Chester county; near the Gulf, and in Plymouth and Whitemarsh townships, in Montgomery county; and a large profitable business is carried on at these places, but as they do not properly belong to my subject, I shall make no further observations upon them. While the manufacture of iron was carried on at Valley Forge, the pigs were obtained from various parts of Berks and Chester counties, where the Potts family held several valuable furnaces.

The great source of mineral wealth in that portion of country that has been described, lying on the eastern side of the Schuylkill and the Valley Creek, consists in immense bodies of limestone, lying on the Schuylkill and in the Great Valley. These, in many places, have been, particularly within the last thirty years, improved to great advantage by the owners of them, and have proved a twofold source of profit, not only to them, but to all portions of the country where agriculture has been benefitted by the application of lime as a manure, thus enriching both the vender and the purchaser.

Having already said much on that subject in some former numbers, I shall dismiss the subject by observing that to see the various operations in this line of business, would amply repay the man of leisure to visit the place. In addition to the limestone, building stone of a valuable quality abounds on almost all of this property, particularly those lying on the river. Since the property known as Headquarters has been owned by James Jones, free stone of an excellent quality has been found upon it, and large quantities of the article have been sent by boats to Philadelphia and other places for buildings of different kinds. On a part of the property formerly belonging to David Stephens (now Isaac Richardson) clay for the manufacture of crucible for the use of brass foundries has been obtained, but never to any great extent.

As noticed in the commencement of this letter, large quantities of copper have been discovered in that section of country lying on the western side of the Valley Creek, in Chester county. On account of this discovery, Remington & Co. have purchased large portions of land in this district; and I have understood, on some of the property purchased by them, rich veins, yielding at the rate of seventy per cent. have been found within fifteen feet of the surface, and that successful operations in that line are now being conducted. I have never yet visited them to be able to convey correct information from actual observation and enquiry. I, therefore, make this statement from such information as I have received from others in whose reports I could rely. I have seen some specimens of this mine, but have never had any in my possession. I have likewise understood that the operations of mining, in the manner that they are conducted, are objects worthy of a visit, and intend, as soon as possible, if nothing intervenes to prevent, to endeavor to accomplish it. The greatest body and most profitable vein of copper, I have been informed, has been found on a farm in Schuylkill township, Chester county, about two miles northwest of Valley Forge. How far similar discoveries in other places have been made, I have not learned; but one thing is certain, that these discoveries had a tendency to enhance the value of land, and the company last alluded to have, within the present year, purchased, at an advanced price, all the land they could obtain in the immediate neighborhood of these discoveries, and it is sincerely to be hoped that their prospect may be fully realized and ultimately crowned with success.

On the western side of the Schuylkill, near the lead mines of Perkiomen, similar operations are now in progression. These I believe are carried on by Pedrick & Co., on some of the property of the Wetherill family, but to what extent or with what prospect of success I have not understood, I only state this from report.

Whether or not gold will ever be discovered, I cannot tell, neither is it a matter of great moment to any whether it ever is found, as the pursuit of it would interfere with the habits of industry. It is but a few years since this precious metal was supposed to have been found, but it proved a failure. A black man had purchased a barren and broken spot of land for the purpose of putting up a house upon it. In digging the cellar, he found among the earth, particles resembling brass filings, and also found similar ones among the sand at the bottom of a small stream of water that passed through it. These he and some other persons supposed, when first discovered, to be gold dust; and for a short time it produced considerable excitement, and large offers were made for his lot, but he declined selling; but it was soon found, upon strict investigation, that it turned out to be nothing more than mica, and thus ended the discovery of gold in that quarter. The discovery of the copper is of more recent date.

In two more communications I expect to finish these narratives, and these will be principally confined to relating some circumstances that have taken place in connection with the encampment ground, the most of which have come under my immediate notice, and taken place since my recollection. These things will claim the attention of my next letter; and as I commenced with an introductory, I expect to conclude with a valedictory.

LETTER XXXI

GENERAL REVIEW

AS I contemplate concluding these narratives in my next letter, I shall devote the most of the present one to taking a general review of the old encampment ground, and endeavor to give some further information concerning it, in addition to that already furnished, believing this to be the better way of conveying it to the public. In some of my former letters, I noticed that when the army took possession of the place principally occupied as the encampment ground, it was mostly a dense forest, heavily set with timber, consisting generally of hickory, various kinds of oak, and other timber common to the native forests of that section of country. Nearly all the land lying between the front and rear lines, and the northeastern and southwestern limits of the lines of the encampment was thus circumstanced. The farms of David Stephens, and the two next below him on the river, were the only properties within these prescribed lines that had any buildings upon them at the time. There was also at the time a portion of cleared land, about seventy acres, belonging to my grandfather, within these limits, since disposed of to John Havard, that was cultivated, but there were no buildings upon it.

NEW TIMBER GROWTH

It is hardly necessary again to say that the timber was all destroyed by the army. After the departure of the army, as noticed in former numbers, the greater part of the land that had been previously cleared and cultivated, was again enclosed for agricultural purposes, but much the greater portion of what had been timber land, was left to lie without enclosure for many years, some of it even to the present time. In the course of a short time, the timber commenced growing upon it with great rapidity, being much more heavily set with young and thrifty sprouts, than it had been before it was destroyed. The soil being naturally good, it was in summer well set with grass, which afforded abundant pasturage for the numerous herds of cattle, sheep, and sometimes horses, that were turned upon it by the inhabitants generally to graze at that time, when large portions of land could only with great difficulty be fenced for farming. It also remained an accommodation to numbers for many years after, as I experimentally know. While penning these lines they recall to my mind, the scenes of my youth and my childhood, and the many happy hours that were then spent, and that I have passed in them when alone, barefooted, and rudely clad in native homespun. I have been engaged in hunting cows and horses upon these grounds, where these remains of the sufferings of the people were then visible, and could be viewed without fear or danger; for peace with her olive branch, had driven out the demon of war with all his horrors; the sword had been exchanged for the ploughshare, and the spear for the pruning hook; and often upon these occasions have I been accompanied with an intimate acquaintance of mine from the city of Philadelphia, about a year younger than myself, who used sometimes to spend his summer vacations in our family, and who, though young at the time, used to take great interest in viewing these things, and listening to the relations that were given by my father and mother, of that period. In our rambles on these occasions, in examining the remains of the encampment, and searching for relics of that period to more fully remind us of that time, and to preserve them as mementos of it. The remembrance of these things carries me back in retrospection to that period, and leads me involuntarily to exclaim, Oh, happy days, now past and gone forever, no more to be recalled in this state of being—days of my youth, when perplexing cares and disquietude came not near my dwelling, when earth's engrossing cares and entanglements were strangers, and the ingratitude of man to his fellow-man was unknown, and when I had not fully and experimentally realized the truth of the language of the poet:

> "What is friendship but a name,
> A charm that lulls to sleep,
> A shade that follows wealth and fame
> But leaves the wretched weep."

But why indulge these morbid feelings?—enough of these reflections. Disappointments, distress, and tribulations of various kinds, are the common lot of mankind, and ever will remain to be. But where is the friend of my youth, who used to ramble with me over these grounds? Death has long since called him hence, more than twenty years since he paid the last debt of nature. I mention not his name. He was a youth of bright talents, improved by education, and flattering prospects in the world; and as he grew up to manhood, was the life and source of entertainment among his friends and acquaintance; his company was sought after and courted in the fashionable world, on account of his wealth and accomplishments; but, alas! having nothing beyond these to rely upon, he became the victim of intemperance, and while young in years, he sank into an inebriate's grave.

But to resume the subject. The growth of the timber was

very rapid, and none of the land that was cleared at that time was cultivated for agricultural purposes, woodland being considered of greater value, and a sparse population, it was suffered to grow up. I first remember traversing this ground, in the fall of the fifth year of my age, in company with my two older brothers, to gather chestnuts. This was about twenty-two years after the timber had been destroyed. The chestnut and hickory trees had grown sufficiently large to produce an abundance of nuts; and that with other timber growing upon it, was then being cut for fuel and rail timber. It also abounded with native grapes, and large quantities were annually gathered from what was called the camp. It used to be a common thing for parties of both sexes to be formed to go hunting them. On these occasions it used to be customary for the men and boys to climb the small trees and saplings, and bend them down, and the company then unite in gathering the grapes. But this employment has now ceased; the cupidity of man has now leveled the greater part of this extensive forest, and it is now enclosed and raising agricultural products.

While on the subject, I may mention one of these freaks of nature, or changes in kinds of timber which sometimes takes place upon a second growth; this is evident on this ground. I have understood that previous to the Revolution, very little chestnut timber grew on that part of the ground cleared off by the army, on the eastern side of the Valley Creek. Since that time large portions of chestnut and other timber not then growing upon it, has since grown there, while the native timber previous to that time, has been comparatively small. This change in the growth of the timber was noticed by the late Judge Peters, of the county of Philadelphia; he published an account of it in the Archives of Useful Knowledge. He was encamped there during the time of its destruction, and had seen it previous; upon visiting it some time after he was forcibly struck with the changes of the timber that was then growing upon it.

PILGRIMAGES AND GATHERINGS

The ground occupied by the army encamped there, has always been an object of attraction, and, as such, has often been visited by various persons. Many a venerable patriot, who composed a a part of that Spartan Band encamped there, has in his old days travelled miles to again behold it, and to review the scenes of that suffering period. I have seen some of them thus engaged in visiting the place, and marked the emotion visible in their venerable countenances, and seen the tears trickle down their aged and withered cheeks, when on the verge of the grave, they have looked upon it, and these things have again been called to their remembrance; and remarked the joy that was also manifest when contrasting the happy and prosperous situation, not only of that portion of the country, but the nation at large, with the gloomy state of things they had there witnessed. These have in all probability all gone down to the grave.

In order that the recollections of that period may not be forgotten, associations of various kinds have been held upon the ground; such as military parades, celebrations and political meetings, the most of the latter during several presidential campaigns within the last twenty-five years. I can say but little concerning any of these meetings—nothing from actual observation, though the most of them have occurred since my time; but having never been in the practice of attending any meetings, either political or military (except to exercise my rights of suffrage for civil officers), I shall say but little concerning them. The political meetings were always of a party kind; and on such times care was taken as far as practicable, to collect surviving officers and soldiers of the Revolution to attend. The military parades were generally volunteer companies, who met to drill on what is called the old ground. On one occasion of this kind, when a troop of cavalry that was forming in Chester county met upon the ground, a quarrel ensued between the captain of the company and a Polish exile named La Reuf, who was employed to teach them cavalry tactics. It proved nearly fatal to the latter. Fifty-three years have elapsed, it was before my recollection; but I have often heard the story related by some who had seen the encounter. The captain of that company, who has since filled very important stations in civil government, and been a candidate for other high offices, is still living, being over eighty years of age. Another individual that then belonged to it, near the same age, and living near him, is the only other surviving person present on the occasion.

VISIT OF LAFAYETTE

When Lafayette, as the nation's guest, in the years of 1824 and 1825, was in this country, preparations were made to induce him to visit the Valley Forge, intending, if it could be effected, to welcome him by having a large and enthusiastic meeting upon his arrival. It is unnecessary to say much concerning his visit to this country, as it is well remembered by many of my readers—the flattering reception he met with in all his journey, and the universal respect paid to him on the occasion is not forgotten, as it was then the general topic of conversation, and has since been so often repeated that but few persons are now to be found of sufficient age and observation, but what are conversant with the circumstances of his visit to this country. At this time there was residing in that section of country, several persons then advanced in years, who had been acquainted with him during his abode there at the time of the encampment, who felt desirous of seeing him.

Among this number were my mother and her sister, the late Mary Rossiter, about two years younger. They had been intimately acquainted with him at the time, he having frequently visited De Kalb at their father's house, mingling in social converse with the family on these occasions; for in private life or when released from duty for a short time, he was of a sociable and very agreeable disposition, and highly relished the opportunity thus afforded him of mingling in family circles. This gave them some knowledge of his general character and habits, at least as they were in early life. On this account they wished to see him, if they could have met him as in former times, in their social family circle; and when conversing upon the subject, they observed to one another, after some remarks upon the attention and applause everywhere bestowed upon him, that they were very certain that it would afford him more satisfaction to spend a few hours in social conversation, on the events of the Revolution, the scenes of the encampment, and of Baron De Kalb, and other officers that used to be in company together at their father's during that period, than to be hurried from place to place, to gratify public curiosity, to attend public meetings, and receive the plaudits of the multitude.

In order to ascertain his views on the subject of a visit to the place, a committee was appointed to visit him on the subject, and invite him to visit the spot, once the scene of suffering to him and his companions in arms. One of the number, the late George B. Loundes, who, at the time, resided at Headquarters, had an interview with him at West Chester, and spent about an hour with him in private company. Lafayette inquired concerning the place, the changes it had passed through, its present state, the old encampment ground, and for many of the families residing there at the time with whom he had been acquainted; and, upon finding that there were some of them still remaining in the neighborhood of the place, though like himself, advanced in years, he desired his love affectionately to them all, and regretted that he could not have the opportunity of visiting them; and also, to inform his once young, now old friends, that it would afford him inexpressible satisfaction, if he could be permitted to visit them, at their respective habitations, mingle with them in social converse as in bygone days, and spend a short portion of time with them in retirement from the pomp and ceremony that surrounded him, and visit the old encampment ground, the famed scene of suffering and distress that was indelibly imprinted on his memory; and that it would not only be his desire to do so, but, if it could be accomplished in this manner, he would avail himself of the opportunity. The opportunity was not afforded him, and he could not comply.

The time of his departure to his native land was then near at hand, and he therefore declined a visit to the place, much to the regret of many who desired to see him. For the same reasons he declined a visit to the Honorable Isaac Wayne, at his residence in Easttown township, Chester county, at the mansion occupied by his father, the late General Anthony Wayne. In a former letter, I mentioned that I might give some further notice concerning this place. It is a large and commodious house, that has been in possession of the family for more than an hundred years; an elegant engraving of it, and also a very correct one, may be seen in Sherman Day's historical researches of Pennsylvania, to which my readers are referred. The present occupant and owner, the only son of the General, and the last of the name of that branch of the family, is more than eighty years of age, and, of course, feels the infirmities of age. He has, in his life time, filled numerous offices of trust and responsibility, in the general and state government, and was the unsuccessful candidate for Governor of Pennsylvania in 1814. He and the Hon. Jonathan Roberts, near the same age, and known by the stations he has filled in public life, and who resides in Upper Merion township, about five miles from Valley Forge, are all the persons I know of now living within that distance of the place, that were of sufficient age at the time of the encampment to remember the transaction of it; and they must, ere long, cease to be amongst us.

This communication has been extended to an unusual length, and I must now conclude for the present; and in my next, if possible, draw the whole subject to a conclusion.

LETTER XXXII

CONCLUSION

I RESUME my pen in order to commence my last communication on the subject that has so long occupied our attention. Much more might have been said upon it, as I have obtained some further information since their publication, from a few aged persons whom I have met, but as the proper time for inserting them has passed, I, therefore, shall reluctantly omit them, and proceed to a conclusion.

I may here remark that an intimate female friend of mine, residing in the borough of Doylestown, enquired of me whether I would conclude with a heroine to my story. This request, I understood, was made at the suggestion of others of the borough. In answer to the inquiry and request, I may inform them that it was not my intention to introduce any works of fiction or romance in these narratives, and I shall adhere to it. All that has been inserted are facts that I have heard related, or that have transpired under my immediate notice, and as such, have endeavored to give a full and impartial narrative concerning them. It is true there may have some errors occurred in relating the history, but I trust nothing material, and they may be overlooked. If any of my readers desire a hero or heroine to complete these sketches, I think they can find them in the true accounts given of my mother's journey to hunt Jehu, and the female friend alluded to who rereleased her husband from York prison: these accounts, with a little further addition concerning the sequel of their lives may answer for heroines to my history. I shall, therefore, proceed to give a few more additional particulars concerning them.

HEROINES OF THE HISTORY

The latter, who released her husband, soon after her arrival in Philadelphia, was, with other Americans who favored the royal cause, sent to England. After a residence there of several years, they removed to Nova Scotia, and from thence to Montreal in Canada. At the latter place, I think, her husband died, and she, with her family, removed to the neighborhood of Spring Garden township, in Chester county; where, sometime after, she married the person at whose house they arrived the morning after their flight from York, he having, in the meantime, become a widower.

She then removed to reside with him at the place where she spent the residue of her days, a useful and highly esteemed member of the religious Society of Friends, a kind neighbor and affectionate mother, and, after having fulfilled these various duties, she closed a useful and exemplary life in a good old age, in the spring of 1813.

To complete the story of my heroine, I hope I may be excused if I pay a small tribute to my parents, from whom I received the greater part of the foregoing accounts concerning the Revolution. In the first place, though not properly in the order of time, yet to connect the matter now engaged, I shall give the sequel of the life of my worthy mother. She was one, born and died on the same spot of earth, and her long life was attended with many vicissitudes, and had to encounter many severe hardships and trials through her long life, particularly about the period of the Revolution, and her four days eventful journey mentioned in my fourth and fifth numbers, may be taken as a sample of what she and many others, similarly situated, had to pass through; but possessing strong powers of mind and health of body, she was enabled to persevere through all; and though fortune smiled not upon her, and disappointment and distress often marked her passing through life, yet she attained a great age, retaining to the last her mental faculties and memory, though for several years of her life deprived of the blessings of sight and hearing, and in other respects much debilitated, yet her recollection was vivid, and having the use of her conversational powers and a happy facility in conveying her sentiments, her company, even in old age, was very interesting. She abounded in anecdotes, reminiscences and historical facts of the period of the Revolution, particularly the time of the encampment; and having been intimately acquainted with Washington, DeKalb, Lafayette, Wayne, Greene, Mifflin, Sullivan, and many others of the general officers of that period, she was often visited by persons of all ages and both sexes, who were eager to obtain information concerning those times; so much so that she used frequently to observe, in a jocose manner, that she believed people considered her a history of the encampment at Valley Forge. Her death occurred, on the same farm on which she was born and lived the greater part of her life, a little more than three years since, in the eighty-ninth year of her age.

I hope to be indulged, if I, in this place, make a few remarks concerning my father. Although his death occurred many years before my mother's, yet I have placed it here in order to place the accounts of my heroines in connection. My father, if living at this time (1850), would have been one hundred years old. The early part of his life, previous to joining the army, and till near its close, was spent in various places, both on sea and land. The place of his nativity was in the state, then colony, of Maryland;

and I have heard him relate many incidents of his early life. He was left an orphan when very young, and never had any knowledge of his parents or family connections. He left that country when young and never returned to it. Among other things related, I have heard him mention his having seen, when young, General Braddock with his army land at Annapolis. After some time spent in various places, he settled, when young, in Hillsborough, in the state of North Carolina. While residing there he was one of a number of young men who accompanied Daniel Boone and Henderson to Kentucky. Soon after this expedition, he entered the army, and continued in it till near the close of the war. He finally settled, about forty years before his death, at the place where a part of our family still reside, where he spent the remainder of his days. He was deprived of life by a fatal accident, on the 23d of twelfth month, (December) 1820, aged seventy-one years. In addition to what I have heard him relate concerning the encampment at Valley Forge that has been inserted, much more might have been added concerning that particular time, but it must be omitted. And if time afforded me the opportunity of embodying in language the various accounts of his early life, the incidents of the Revolution that he witnessed, the many battles and marches he engaged in, and also some events of his subsequent life, it would afford material for several months publication in similar communications to this and the preceding ones, and furnish some additional historical facts concerning the Revolution, that have never been published, but I shall now take leave of the subject and draw towards a close.

Having now given a history of all the farms that were in the immediate vicinity of Valley Forge, particularly those that were embraced in the lines of the encampment, and such as were the theatre of important and interesting events during that period, and in some of my former letters have had reference to the early settlement of some of them, the state of things at the time of the Revolution, the tried situation of the inhabitants during that period, the quarters of the different general officers, the desolate state of the country after the removal of the army, its improvement since that time, also its present situation and owners, and likewise the discoveries of various mineral substances that have recently been discovered in that section of country, I am sensible that many of these things may not be of sufficient interest to many persons unacquainted with the localities of the place, and the families and persons who have been alluded to. I have, therefore, inserted them that should any who are strangers to them visit that portion of country, they may, upon inquiry, ascertain the different places referred to in the preceding communications; and I hope they will accept of these last remarks as an excuse for their publication, if any be necessary.

In preparing this account of a portion of country intimately connected with our national existence, and identified with the history of the Revolution, I am aware of not doing justice to the subject and of embodying it in language as clear and comprehensive as I could have wished for the information of my numerous readers, not only of the papers of this county, but in many other places I have been informed these documents have been published, yet I hope I shall so far succeed in my undertaking as to induce some among those who never have, to visit the place and behold what I have endeavored to describe.

I would, therefore, request those who have leisure and inclination to visit the place. A few hours ride from the borough of Doylestown would convey them there, a journey that would amply repay their toil. At Port Kennedy they would find an excellent hotel, furnished with every accommodation. In traveling the country many traces of the encampment would be found, to remind them of the troublesome times our ancestors passed through to purchase our freedom. And those who witnessed that period would not be met with, as these are nearly all gone down to the grave, and the few survivors are far advanced in years, and none residing in the immediate vicinity, yet in their rambles they would meet with many to whom these things are known, among whom are some of the descendants of the Moores, the Stephenses, the Walkers and other families which have been noticed, who still would delight to point out the situations, localities, objects and improvements that have been mentioned.

It is not, as in a former letter, in imagination but in reality, that I now request some of my readers who have never visited these places to visit the place, and first to stand upon the spot once known as Mordecai Moore's fort, and from this eminence view the portion of country that I have been describing—once a scene of desolation from the effects of the encampment, and where many a patriot of the Revolution suffered more than language can describe, from the cold, chilling wind and driving snows, and other accumulated sufferings, already noticed, and while you figure to your imagination the state of things then existing there, contrast it with its now prosperous condition. On every side as far as the sight extends, is seen the marks of industry exhibited in a highly cultivated country, large buildings and fruitful abounding with plenty and teeming with flocks and herds. On the south and east will be seen the fruitful farms of the Great Valley, exceeded by few, in any, in the state, and on the north and west the beautiful Schuylkill and Reading Railroad, the former majestically bearing on its placid bosom its large boats laden with coal, lime and numerous other products; the latter with the numerous pleasure and burden cars, propelled by locomotives, freighted in like manner and moving with incredible velocity from one place to another; while near upon the Schuylkill may be seen the thriving village of Port Kennedy, and also see and behold the hum of business carried on at the place. In addition to these artificial improvements, may be beheld on both sides of the river nature's scenery equally beautiful and interesting, that while gazing on on these things the viewer will be almost involuntarily led to exclaim with Dyer in his poetic description of "Grouger Hill," nearly as follows:

"Ever charming, ever new—
When will the landscape tire the view;
The 'river,' village, dome and farm,
Each gives each a double charm."

From this place traverse the old encampment ground; view the remains of the fortifications and the breastworks and the outlines of the huts, visit Headquarters at Valley Forge, view the different manufactories of the place, the copper mines in the vicinity, the lime kilns at Port Kennedy, and many other things that may be found in the limits of that section of country, which has been described, but which time would fail me to enumerate, and which must be seen to be duly appreciated. I, therefore, leave them for the further personal examination of any who feel sufficiently interested in the subject to visit them, fully persuaded that few, if any, would regret their visit. I shall now proceed to

AUTHOR'S VALEDICTORY

In drawing these narratives to a conclusion I may acknowledge the flattering accounts I have received of their reception, not only in this my adopted county, but in other parts of the country, and in the halls of our National Legislature. It confirms me in an opinion that I entertained in the commencement of the work, that the subject is one of deep interest, and worthy of being rescued from oblivion. And this small section of country will always occupy a conspicuous place in the history of our national existence. In this, our large and vastly extended Republic, there are, no doubt, in the greater part of it the descendants of those who were there during that gloomy period, and to whom they will prove interesting, and recall to their memories many things that they have heard related by those who witnessed these things. But I regret that it was not undertaken at an earlier period, particularly while my friend, the late Matthias Holstein, of Norristown, was living, who was always desirous that these accounts should be preserved and given to the public, and who urgently requested me to undertake it. His death occured before I commenced the collection, which I deferred for a considerable time, hoping an able writer, who was in possession of the same and more materials for the compilation of a work of this kind, would have undertaken it. I may also add that I have been frequently solicited of late to have them published in a volume, in order more fully to preserve them. And the question is often asked whether it will be done. In reply, I can only say at present, that the manuscripts will be preserved, but if they should ever be published, it will be necessary for them to undergo a revision, as many of them were written in haste, and sent to the printer without previous correction, which may account for many errors and omissions, as well as grammatical constructions in the publication of different communications. Should they ever be published in a volume, some extraneous matter and repetitions will be omitted, and considerable additional information, some of which was purposely omitted in order to make the account as short as possible, and some that has been furnished since commencing the publication, but not received in proper time, will be inserted.

While penning this last communication my mind is clothed with serious impressions, when thought carries me back to the Revolution, and memory brings to my recollection those who were then the owners or occupants of that land that was the scene of the events that have been described. The most of them I remember, but more than thirty years have rolled around since the last of them have gone down to the grave; and of their children there are but three of them left remaining, and these are more than four score years of age. Myself and the contemporaries of my youthful days, who still survive, are now growing old, and in a quarter of a century more how few of us will be in this state of existence; the most of us will be mouldering in the dust, and our children and grandchildren will fill our places. We cannot look into futurity and behold the future destiny of our now prosperous and happy country, but when we look back on the last quarter of a century, how are we struck with admiration and amazement, when we see the great advancement and the many improvements that have taken place during that period. And how great has been the extent of our country, and the increase of population since the adoption of our present Constitution. Our territory and population are no longer confined to the original thirteen states, and the limited territory we then possessed. It now extends from the Atlantic to the Pacific Ocean, and from the British possessions on the north and east, to the Mexican on the south, —the most of it abounding with inhabitants, moral and intelligent, all members of this great Republic, and equally interested in its preservation. All these acquisitions which it is needless to detail, and the many improvements that we see around us have taken place since the commencement of the present century, and are still moving onward. Who can calculate the advancement they may continue to make in a few years, if they continue to progress in the same ratio—what the youth of the present generation will live to behold when we are no more!

The perpetuation of our free institutions, the cultivation of universal peace with all nations, the subject of general education, the acquirement of industrious and correct habits, are subjects next to our gratitude to the Great Author of all good for the many blessings we enjoy ought to claim our serious consideration, in order that they may descend as rich legacies to our latest posterity.

And let us ever remember the hardships and sufferings our predecessors passed through in order to obtain it, a part of which may be learned by perusing the foregoing narrative. It was by being united they obtained it, and by continuing united it will be preserved. And by contrasting the present state of our country, and the changes that have taken place since the period of the Revolution, and when we view its present happy and prosperous condition compared with the gloomy state of things then existing, let it teach us to value the blessings of peace and industry, and fondly hope that it will ever continue to dwell in our land and the day arrive when "nation shall not lift up the sword against nation, and the sons of men learn war no more."

In taking leave of my readers, and concluding the subject, I may remark, that when I review what I have been writing, and contemplate the changes that have taken place since my recollection, and when thought carries me back to that time when the foot of civilized man never had trod the ground that had been described, recur to its early settlement, and lastly reflect upon the number of my friends and acquaintances of all ages and different periods, that since my time have been laid in the dust, I am forcibly reminded of one of the poetic effusions of my early friend and associate, Charles W. Thomson, now Rector of the Episcopal Church at York, in this state, entitled the "Islet of Ona," a poetic name given by him to a small island in the Schuylkill, near Fairmount, on which the lines were written by him, containing a description of the surrounding country previous to its being settled by civilized inhabitants, and contrasting it with its then present state, and alluding to its primitive settlers and its original inhabitants, who had been numbered wth the dead, he concluded with the following lines, that so correspond with my present feelings, that I know of nothing more appropriate for me to conclude this my last communication with. They are as follows:

"And when another century,
As unperceived has passed away—
Fleeting from day to day:
Alas! the scene must shift again
And we who now our seats retain,
Will sleep as sound as they."

APPENDIX

EDWARD WOODMAN. FATHER OF THE HISTORIAN

A sketch by his granddaughter, Miss Mary S. Woodman, for his descendants.

EARLY LIFE

It may be said that Edward Woodman is the first one of the family we know of with any certainty. He was born in Chestertown, Md., on Christmas Day, 1749. His parents, whose Christian names are not known by the writer, were of English origin or direct from England. But it is supposed they were descendants of the New England pioneers that settled at Newburyport, Mass., and were among the settlers. (A genealogy written by Cyrus Woodman, one of the New England Woodmans, gives a very interesting account of them down to the present day. They were a sturdy and upright people.)

His father, he was told, died in August, before his birth. His mother landed at Chestertown soon after the death of her husband, which occurred at sea. From what has been told the writer, it is safe to conclude his parents had previously established a home at Chestertown. His earliest remembrance of himself was living with his mother, an old negress and a negro lad at Chestertown. His mother died when he was quite young. He could remember his baptism in the Episcopal church. Whether his mother was living at the time is not known. After the death of his mother, he was taken into the family of William Clayton, also the two negroes. The old woman curled his hair and dressed him, besides other things needful in the care of a child. All the comforts of that early time were bestowed upon the little orphan boy. A pony was kept for his sole use. When the boy Edward was old enough to go to school, the pony was saddled and he rode it, the negro boy walking along side, carrying a basket with his dinner in it. When the school closed for the day, the negro came with the pony to take him back to the Clayton home. The negro boy often told him he owned the old woman and himself, and that they did not belong to Master William Clayton. From the care taken of him by the two slaves, and many other attentions he received, we suppose he was the owner of property, real or personal, and that William Clayton was the guardian.

Things went well with the boy while William Clayton lived. Judging from the many things he used to tell of boyish tricks and pranks of which he was guilty, not sinful but annoying to those who had to live with him, he certainly was not always a pleasure to the Clayton family. William Clayton and his wife were very kind to him at all times, Mrs. Clayton often taking him with her when she went on horseback to visit her friends. He was on his pony, one or more of the daughters on their ponies, all going on a visit, where he was given a full share of all the pleasures of the table and household. How long William Clayton lived after he took his ward into his family I cannot say. He was a kind man to all his family and slaves. To his daughters and the orphan whom he sheltered he was over indulgent, at least so the boy thought after he came to the mature thoughts of manhood. He used afterwards to say sometimes, "What a spoiled, careless, disagreeable boy I must have have been!"

FOUR YEARS WITH PIRATES

Time, which brings changes to all things, brought a great change to young Edward. When he was thirteen or fourteen years old, he did not remember the exact age at the time, he took life into his own management. William Clayton was dead but he was still with the widow and daughters. The girls scolded him so much and so often he got tired of it, so concluded to run away.

Clayton owned a ship that traded between Chestertown and the Island of Barbadoes. The ship was back from a voyage and loading for another. A good opportunity thought the boy, so off he went, the thoughtless, misguided little fellow. The sailors hid him from the captain, till the ship was so far out that he could not be put ashore. On the return voyage the captain thought to add still more to the profits, either for the Clayton family or for himself. So he sailed to Virginia, disposed of his cargo, reloaded and set sail again, bound for Halifax. The breezes may have been good, and the skies fair, but fortune was not so kind. When only a few days out, they were run down, captured and robbed of such things as were wanted by a ship that had sailed under letters of marque, authorized by the English government to prey upon the French during the French and Indian War in Canada. The war being over, the captain and the crew banded themselves into a perfectly lawless set, that lived by stealing on land and sea whatever they could without danger to themselves. What became of Clayton's ship, captain or crew, I am unable to say further than that they were allowed to go unhurt. But the young wayfaring boy was taken from it and put on board the pirate vessel. After getting enough for their wants awhile, they would go to some remote part of the West Indies or elsewhere. When it was consumed, out again for another voyage of plunder twice going south of the equator. Though theft was the means by which they lived, no murder or other outrage was committed. They were simply vagabonds on sea. Little Ned was not asked to do anything he did not wish to, was treated with kindness at all times, but the life of a half pirate did not accord with his nature. Nature will under adverse conditions, in part if not entirely, assert itself. So in the case of the captive boy a secret desire was ever present in his mind to get away from his dishonest captors. Four years passed before the opportunity came to escape.

The ship was sailing off the coast of North Carolina. In some way it became unseaworthy and put into one of the ports of that colony. Seeing his time had come, he made good his escape, and ran back into the thinly settled parts of the country, and worked for the settlers till he felt safe in going to the more populous parts of the colony. So far as there is any account of his life in North Carolina, he lived in several different places. At one time he lived at or near New Garden, a settlement of Friends from New Garden, Chester county, Pa. On another occasion Col. Henderson (see history of North Carolina) was collecting supplies to fill a treaty with the Indians of the frontier. He took fifty men, each furnished with a horse to ride. The horse, in addition to carrying the rider, was loaded with a large saddle-bag, in each end of which was a little keg of rum and small trinkets for the Indians. Still more each man led two pack horses loaded with blankets, knives and other things. Edward Woodman was one of these men. Daniel Boone was the guide and assistant of Col. Henderson.

THE BATTLE OF MOORE'S CREEK BRIDGE

The family accounts of my grandfather are so fragmentary, I write with constant fear my history may not be correct or properly connected. At one time he lived in Tyrell county. On the outbreak of the Revolution-

THE HISTORY OF VALLEY FORGE 159

ary War, his home was near Hillsboro, where, in company with many others of the patriots, he was drilling for whatever service they might be called on to perform. The officers under whom the patriots were enlisted were Gen. Moore and Col. Caswell. One day when they were at work in the fields, a company came saying they were organizing with all possible speed and were to repair to the home of Col. Caswell, near what is now Fayetteville, N. C. He ungeared "the critters" (horses), gave them to the charge of a black boy at work with him, at the same time telling him to go in the house and say to the women folks that when he came back he would bid them good-bye. Little did or could he foresee the many privations and hardships before him or that he would never see the women folks again.

The cause for the sudden calling together of the minute men was to intercept a body of Scotch and Irish settlers, together with the Tories to the number of 1500, under the command of Major Gen. McCloud and Brig.-Gen. McDonald. A correspondence had been carried on between Sir. Henry Clinton at New York and Gen. McCloud. Their plan was for Clinton to send a fleet that should sail up the Cape Fear river to Wilmington and there land. McCloud would there join Sir Henry's men, and the united forces were then to march throughout the colony and subdue the patriots and thus secure N. C. to the English.

The enemy met with no opposition till one day's march from Wilmington. Gen. Moore being apprized from the first, unknown to McCloud, was watching his movements from the rear. Caswell with 900 men went ahead and placed them in ambush on the opposite side of the bridge spanning Moore's Creek. The bridge was reached through a long narrow defile of hills on each side that prevented retreat. General McCloud, dressd in Highland, uniform, as were also his men, came riding on the bridge, waved his sword and called on his men to follow. Half the flooring of the bridge on the side on which the patriots lay had been removed. At that point McCloud halted. On the instant Col. Caswell opened fire, killing General McCloud and all who were on the bridge. Gen. McDonald rallied the men and fired, but with no effect, Caswell's men being so well protected by tall trees and underwood. Caswell returned the fire with such deadly effect and the enemy lost so heavily that Gen. McDonald soon made a complete surrender. Officers and men took oath not to engage again against the colonists. All were sent under guard to their homes except 300 Scotchmen, who were held as hostages and exchanged for our men who were confined on prison ships.

WOODEN PINS FOR FORT MOULTRIE

The battle of Moore's Creek Bridge, Feb. 27, 1776, marks the time when Edward Woodman entered the American army. The next active service he saw was when the British fleet appeared off Charleston, S. C., and attacked the fortifications on Sullivan's Island, June 4, 1776. Edward was one of the soldiers who helped build Fort Moultrie, the palmetto logs being fastened together with wooden pins which he and nineteen others had been detached to make. He was not given to boasting but was always proud of having been one of the twenty men who made the wooden pins.

OFF TO THE NORTH

As soon as the British sailed away, the division to which he was attached was ordered to march north. After marching thirty days over bad roads, much of the way only horse paths, many of the men had died from heat and fatigue. The horses became so lame that the men walked much of the way. They could get plenty to eat. "The time for empty stomachs," he used facetiously to say, "had not yet come," at the same time giving a merry wink with his bright blue eyes. When they had reached within one day's march of Boston, they were turned and sent to Long Island, where Washington met a serious defeat. He saw much hard fighting and skirmishing on Long Island. The officers under whom he came north cannot be named, but they were now attached to Washington's army, and for the greater number of the ensuing years shared all the hardships and privations of that heroic band of officers and men.

THE BATTLE OF TRENTON

In the late autumn of 1776 Washington was encamped on the bank of the Delaware river, upon Jericho Hill, near McConky's Ferry, in Bucks county, Penn. The army was much reduced in numbers, owing to much discontent among the soldiers, caused largely by their poor clothing and not having been paid money due them. Many whose term of enlistment had expired returned to their homes. Our brave grandfather remained firm and true to the cause of Independence. On that memorable night of Christmas, 1776, Washington crossed the Delaware at McConky's Ferry, now known as Taylorsville. Of this crossing into New Jersey we all know the results "from the books we have read." Gen. Sullivan crossed ahead of his men. When his horse was over, he mounted and sat silently watching his soldiers till all were over. Then, taking a pinch of snuff, he said, "Come on, boys." And onward they went through darkness and snow.

An incident occurred that night which was the experience of one or more of Edward Woodman's friends (they had likes and dislikes among their comrades), a memory of whom held a place in his heart through life. Though the greater part of the army crossed at McConky's Ferry, two companies went up to Coryell's Ferry (New Hope), where they ferried across. Having first to go up the river and then down in the darkness and snow, daylight came before they reached Trenton. At length they came upon a better road and all took to running. When nearing Trenton the officer called a halt and told them to slow and to form in line so as to be ready for action. After going forward a few hundred yards in good order, they saw and heard three fifers coming to meet them playing, "White Cockade and Peacock Feather, American Boys Fight Forever." The music told the victory, the line broke immediately. Every man felt tired and hungry, a feeling he had not thought of before he saw the fifers. A more limp and lazy set of soldiers never before marched into a place of victory. If any of their descendants desire to know in what part of the capture of Trenton grandfather participated, by consulting history and finding the part of Gen. Sullivan, it can be known. That was the command he was under. After the capture of Trenton and the Battle of Princeton, he was still alive, still sharing the privations and hardships of his patriotic comrades.

A HORSE'S BREATH

There is another incident connected with his army life that may come in here, as I do not know where he was at the time it occurred. Winter was approaching. An officer with a small squad of soldiers was sent to examine a place which lay some miles distant from where the army was encamped, the object being to search for a good situation for winter quarters. One blanket, a gun and some ammunition was all they carried with them. After a day of more than usual fatigue, they lay down on the ground with their guns beside them, all near together to keep warmer. It was already dark. The officer and men were sure there were no British in the neighborhood. So sure were they, no guard was placed over them, a great mistake, for one of the men awoke in the night and going a little distance from the others, found they were surrounded by British horsemen. The order was "Every man run and save his life as he can." Grandfather had not run far when he felt the breath of a horse against his face. Turning around he saw the rider bending forward to strike him with his sword. Being too quick for him, he ran his bayonet into his assailant's abdomen. The man gave a scream, turned his horse and rode away. Aunt Ruth said her father always spoke of the events of that time with sadness. He would say, "That poor man was the only person I ever knew to a certainty I killed." Running on he came to a woods and going into it a short distance he found himself on a steep hill. Knowing he could not be followed, he hunted for a big tree and sat down on the sheltered side with his back to the trunk, and was soon asleep. On waking in the morning (as he thought) the sun was up. Looking around he saw only a few feet from where he had spent the night a high rocky bank with a deep creek at the bottom. Again his life had been spared by not falling over and drowning. Coming from another direction and leading down the hill was a well trodden path. Following it he saw two sets of farm buildings on the other side of the creek. After walking more than a mile he came upon foot-stones. The path led up to one of the farm houses, where they gave him his supper and shelter for the night. The sun was almost set. He had slept in the woods nearly the whole day. When the sun had risen in the morning, it had shone through the leafless trees and warmed him so he slept till after noon. The house was filled with women and children, the men of both families being in the American army. The women and children, from a grandmother to a nursing child, were living together to help each other as best they could. The other house was abandoned. Morning came and he was about to leave, when one of the women said: "Soldier, you are numbered with the dead. Stay and work for us; we need your help so much." He had told them how he came to be there and of the skirmish in the night. The offer was good, the summer campaign was over, so he stayed and worked hard in preparing material for a fence which the women and children could build in the spring. He was well clothed and fed, even had stockings and shoes, the only ones he ever got during his whole term of service in the Revolution. The shoes he had on when first sent north wore out on the march and he afterward went barefoot with the one exception. He did not suffer so much as many of his comrades, whose feet often cracked and bled. It was his practice often to wash his feet, which he thought was the cause of their always being so sound and well.

Spring came and the one whose life we are trying to follow turneu his mind again to what he felt to be his greatest duty. Taking his gun one morning in March and bidding the family farewell, he trudged off to the army again. On reaching the encampment he asked to see Gen. Sullivan. The officer who received him asked many questions. What had he come there for? Why must he see Gen. Sullivan? etc., etc. Handing the officer his gun, he answered: "Search me well, see that I have nothing with which to injure the commander, and take me to him. I have something to say to him I can say to no one else." To Sullivan he was sent, and he told his story—how he had escaped in the night and where the winter was spent, and gave his reasons for not returning sooner. "Now the time is come I might be needed. Here I am, you see." The General listened quietly to all he had to say, then answered: "My boy, I am glad you are back and gladder yet you are alive." Then giving him a hearty handshake and a pinch of snuff, he sent him back to his place in the ranks of the army. The reason for insisting to see Sullivan was that if he reported to any other officer, the danger of being treated as a deserter was hanging over him. Sullivan was a man of such nobility of character, no fear was to be apprehended from that score.

It is to be regretted we do not know in what locality the foregoing occurrence happened, but suppose it somewhere in New England. It was so cold the milk froze in their living room. Nor do we know the date of the winter.

AT BRANDYWINE AND GERMANTOWN

In August, 1777, Washington with his army was encamped in Warwick township, Bucks county, Pa. Wm. J. Buck states there were North Carolina troops among them. We suppose our grandfather was there. Family annals tell to a certainty he was in the Battle of Brandywine, Sept. 11, 1777; and also at Germantown, Oct. 3, 1777. In the death of Gen. Nash, which occurred in the latter battle, he suffered what he always felt to be a personal loss. They had been acquainted in North Carolina, and throughout all the changes, hard or easy, that the fortunes of war brought to them, Gen. Nash was his firm friend. Our grandfather was near him when he fell. He was one to help bear him from the field and to bury him in the graveyard belonging to the church at Toamencin, Pa.

AT VALLEY FORGE

Throughout all his wanderings, far or near, there is no place around which so much interest centers or so great a desire is felt by his descendants to know all about him as his coming to Valley Forge, Dec., 1777.

Very soon after the army became encamped, smallpox broke out. Our great-grandfather Abijah Stephens went early every morning to the camp and stayd late in the evening, waiting on the sick. One evening when he came home, he said to his wife: "Priscilla, there is a soldier that helps me to nurse the sick, that came from North Carolina, he told me to-day. He knows thy brother, William Thomas. He has worked for him and other Friends who went from Chester county."

Twice the soldier was brought home by the "Doctor" to see Priscilla, but how long the visits were is not told, though she was well pleased with him on both occasions. After he married her daughter, she became much attached to him. Aunt Ruth said: "Well she might be, for he was faithful in all things, great or small, that added to her comfort or happiness."

In June, 1778, Washington moved the army from Valley Forge; and among the 11,000 the ragged, barefooted soldier, that was in the future to become our grandfather, marched away with no thought or expectation of ever returning.

HIS WAR RECORD

It would be a pleasure to give some of the varying vicissitudes through which, with his comrades in arms, he was destined to pass before fate sent his returning footsteps to the home of Abijah Stephens.

He enrolled himself with the first movement in North Carolina, encountered the first fighting at Moore's Creek Bridge, N. C., under command of Gen. Moore and Col. Caswell. His second term of enlistment expired August, 1782. The long Revolution was nearly over for the Colonies, for him it was ended. The division in which he was serving lay somewhere in the vicinity of New York City. During his campaign of service *he met the enemy 21 times,* some of them skirmishes. At Trenton there was no fighting. At no time was he wounded badly enough to leave the field, though the greater number of the engagements were hard battles, and in several he was exposed to great peril. Neither was he ever sick. Having had the smallpox, he escaped that when it raged with such violence at Valley Forge. Thus we see him leaving the last scenes of war sound and well.

ON THE HOMEWARD WAY

Two others who had enlisted at the same time he did, like him were at liberty to go home. The three started for North Carolina, getting food at the farm houses on the way. One of the men proposed that they go by way of Valley Forge and see how the encampment looked by that time. Grandfather answered: "That is exactly the thing to do. I know Dr. Stephens. He and his wife are benevolent Quakers, a good place to put into for a few days and get rested, fed up and may be clothed." There was a little irony in saying "may be clothed." From the account that comes down of the condition their clothing was in, to be clothed was a foregone necessity.

To all who came to the hospitable home of Abijah Stephens, the latch string hung out. But our returning patriots could not enter when they reached that open door. The miserable rags they wore were so completely worn out, not one of them was fit to appear in the presence of women. The barn afforded a place of refuge. A call brought the men. Food was given them. Grandmother Stephens, whose benevolence knew no bounds and whose generosity never failed, soon had sufficient clothing gathered together for their necessities. Trout Creek was near, no time was lost in availing themselves of its waters. With hair cut and combed, clothed in clean raiment, shaved with a razor (in the army their beards had to be cut with scissors) they went to the house and ate supper with the family off a table. Taking chairs outside they sat around for a friendly talk. It takes little effort of the imagination to suppose their feelings on that evening. It seemed the foreshadow of Paradise.

At the time of which I write, there were many families around the Valley, Radnor, and Newtown Square who had relatives residing in North Carolina. The men were asked to stay till letters could be written for them to take to the friends and relatives so far away. Two weeks passed, the letters were written, the seed wheat they had engaged to thresh was done, the time to go was fixed upon, the morning came, Edward Woodman was sick and not able to go. Both the others had left good homes and parents they were anxious to reach and see. They went on, leaving their companion prostrate at the home of Abijah and Priscilla Stephens. For many days it was thought he would never get well. He never did fully recover a giddiness in his head, which followed the fever. It would attack him at times during his whole life and in the end caused his death. Years after when William Thomas visited his relatives in Chester county, he said the letters were not received, that the men did not reach their homes. They were in all probability takn with the same fever and died on the homeward journey.

After his recovery Edward Woodman worked for different persons. The vicinity of Valley Forge became his home. At one time he worked for ———— Walker, a carpenter. The new-found home that at first seemed only chance proved permanent, and at last became his final resting place. When able to go to work, he left the Stephen's home and did not again become a resident of the household until his marriage gave him an assured place in the family.

A HOME IN THE VALLEY

Edward Woodman and Sarah Stephens were married about five years after he came to Chester Valley. They settled on the little farm that Grandfather Stephens gave them. The land was to be her dower and was taken off the lower end of the Stephen's farm. It was located on the Trout

Run in what is locally known as the Valley. The public road running from Port Kennedy to King-of-Prussia passes through the land.

* * * * * * *

On the morning of Dec. 23, 1820, some persons that lived among the Valley Hills came to the door begging, and went away saying they would be back and get the things. So many demands had been made that season, grandmother felt all she had to give was already gone and had said so to the family at breakfast. Grandfather had finished up the chores about the barn, came to the window calling: "Sally, do not send the poor helpless creatures away from our door empty-handed, they are so needy. Hunt something up to give them."

With a pathos touching to hear, grandmother related to my mother his last words, "Something to give them," adding, "My husband's life was one of service and charity, his last words the expression of his kind benevolent nature." From the window he went to the barn on the Valley Farm to thresh. The sound of the flail was heard at the house but no one noticed it cease. Dinner was ready and Abisha's little son Edward went to call him. He came back saying, grandfather was asleep and would not wake up. The girl went and came back running, having found him on the floor alive but unconscious. He was carried to the house and died in a few minutes. The neighbors on looking saw he had threshed one flooring. Some sheaves lay on the floor for the second. The pitchfork in the mow with a sheaf sticking on the prongs showed beyond doubt he had fallen from the mow to the floor, caused from one of the frequent giddy attacks. The following Christmas would have been his 71st birthday. Friends and relatives held him in such high esteem his funeral procession was a mile long, following on in close line to the Friends' burying ground at the Valley Meeting-house, where all that was mortal of Edward Woodman found final resting place.

HIS PERSONALITY

There was much in the religious Society of Friends he admired. Their outward form suited his tastes, the inner quiet communion suited his spiritual needs. He always wore plain clothes in cut and color, went regularly to meeting on First Days, was particular to pay meeting rates, and to discharge a full share of the necessary work in keeping the grounds around the meeting-house in good order. When asked why he did not become a member, he answered: "That testimony against war keeps me out. I went into the Revolution with a sense of duty and still think it was right."

Aunt Ruth said that in middle life he was erect, nearly six feet tall, with broad shoulders, full chest, fine muscular development throughout, very blue eyes, a sallow complexion, hair light brown and curly, worn brushed back from his forehead and temples and hanging from the crown of his head to his coat collar a mass of curls.

The nieces and nephews have told us of many kind deeds; how he always looked on the bright side of life and had always a smile of welcome and good humored joke when they came to see Aunt Sallie. His daughters said beneath his easy, courteous manner and gayety was a tender conscience, guiding strong religious convictions, which often, when alone with his family, he used to express with beautiful language. They said it was past their understanding how their father could come through the vicissitudes and temptations of his youth and early manhood and keep his morals and integrity, but he did. A soldier who had known him in the army said of him: "His conduct at all times was characterized by courage, manifesting no fear in time of danger. Through cold, hunger and fatigue his cheerfulness never failed, and often raised the drooping spirits of his comrades."

INDEX

Agriculture, 87, 97, 115, 120, 121, 125, 126, 127, 135, 140
American Army, 39, 40, 44, 45, 46, 49, 59, 76
Amiens, Treaty of, 93
Archives of Useful Knowledge, 145
Armstrong, Gen, 58
armory, 86, 103
arms, 31, 89
artillery, 59, 60, 89
Audubon, Joseph, 110
Austria, 70

barns, 75, 120, 121
Barnes, Joseph, 101
Bakewell, Wm., 109
Bakewell sheep, 110
Baptist Road, 27, 37, 60, 111, 112
Baptist meeting-house, 27, 64, 75
Baker, Geo. A., 120
Barry, Samuel, 114
Bartholomew, John, 99
Barren Hill, 45, 89
Beaver, Devault, 115
" Isaac, 128
Beaver, John, 58, 71, 87, 115
Beaver, Margaret, 83
Bean, John, 96
Beidler, Abr., 124
Bethel, Robt., 130
Bilton Line, the, 128
Blackwell, Dr. (Rev.) Robt., 116
Blounts, 65
Blount, Thos., 84
bread, 86
breastworks, 25, 124
Brandywine, 26, 33, 34, 35, 70, 75, 77
British, 24, 30, 31, 33, 34, 36, 37, 38, 41, 42, 43, 45, 46, 47, 60, 61, 64, 88, 89, 90, 91, 99, 120, 121
Brooks, Reese, 101
Brown, John, 53, 58, 111, 112, 115
Brown, Fort, 54
Brooks, Major Wm., 61
Bucks, County of, 26, 28, 94
Bull, John, 36
Burgoyne, Gen., 31, 45, 63, 76
Burr Aaron, 84
burials, 63
Butlers, 65

camp, 45, 54
Campbell, poet, 70

Camden, battle of, 67, 68
Catfish Island, 133
canal, 130, 132, 136
cattle, 41, 55, 121
Chester county, 27, 122
Christ, 25
cavalry, 115
Clinton, Geo., 84
" Dewitt, 85
Cedar Creek, 128
Claibornes, 65
Clever, Gen., 82
clothing, 24, 57, 49, 79
coal, 105
colonists, 42
Columbia Railroad, 60
Commissary Dept., 79
" General, 123
Congress, 46, 62, 63, 64, 72, 79, 99
copper, 108, 125, 138, 139, 141, 142
Conway, Gen., 58, 59, 63, 77
Continental Army, 30, 31, 85, 88, 93
" money, 60, 67, 79, 96, 125
Conshohocken, 60, 89
Conrad, John, 101
" Dennis, 128
cooking, 55
cotton, 103
crops, 75
crystals, 139
Currie, Rev. Wm., 115

Darrach, Lydia, 46, 90
Davis, Geo., 134
" Hon. John, 58, 99
" Dr. Jones, 136
" Joseph, 121
" Mordecai, 121
" Wm., 112, 113
" Zachary, 57, 136
Day's Hist. Researches, 89
Dearborn, Henry, 84
Delaware river, 45
DeKalb, Baron, 58, 64, 67-69, 70, 147, 150
Dennison, Andrew, 94
Dewees, Col. Wm., 31, 32, 37, 38, 42, 43, 97, 99, 120, 121
Dewees, Sarah, 43
" Thomas W., 120
" Waters, 120
" widow, 120, 121

Doylestown, 38
Dubryson, Gen., 58, 70, 71, 97
Duportale, Gen., 60, 70
Duponceau, Gen., 70

Easttown, 77
encampment, 25, 29, 48, 53, 79, 81, 87, 91, 92, 93
encampment ground, 46, 54, 81, 107, 108, 109, 111, 129
Eglington, Mr., 129, 133
Elliot, John, 130
engineers, 60
England, 77, 103
Ephrata, 75
Evan ap Bevan, 28, 122
Evans, Brooks, 103
" Stephen, 28

Fatland Ford, 59, 72
" Island, 133
Fifty Acres, the, 80
Fishbourne, Major Benj., 116, 117
fishing, 129
flour, 87
food, 49, 50, 51, 57, 62, 66, 72
forage, 75
Force, Henry, 57, 133
flocks, 88
Forge, the, 20, 26, 27, 28, 29, 30, 31, 33, 36, 37, 38, 42, 54, 88, 92, 120, 121
forts, 53, 54, 85, 86, 137
Forrest, Thomas, 84
free stone, 140, 141
Frick, John, 130
Fricke, Jacob, 33, 113
fortifications, 25, 111, 123
France, 77
Friends (Quakers), 57, 109, 117, 129, 150
Friends' meeting-house, 75, 76, 80
Front Line Hill, 53, 54, 55, 59, 82, 86, 87, 95, 119, 121, 126
fuel, 74, 75, 79, 88, 89, 92, 95, 96
Furman, Gen., 58

Gates, Gen., 45, 63
Geerhart, Frederic, 87, 105
German farmer, 115
Germantown, 26, 33, 49, 75, 88, 89
Godfrey, Wm., 58, 119
gold, 141, 142
Goshen, 92
Goshen meeting-house, 109
grain, 41
Gray, Col., 30
Green, Lieutenant, 80
Greene, Gen., 58, 64, 76, 116, 118, 150
Greaves, Geo., 119
Griffith, Rev. Abr., 129

grist mill, 100, 125
guards, 83
Gulf Hills, 45, 60, 69
Gulf Road, 27, 37, 59, 60, 80, 89, 100, 103, 131

Hamilton, Col. Alex., 37, 38, 84, 89
hardware, 102, 119
Havard, David, 115
" John, 58, 111, 112, 115, 143
" Samuel, 70, 111, 112
Hazelton, Thomas, 129
Headquarters, 28, 54, 57, 59, 70, 72, 84, 89, 99, 100, 104, 107, 123, 137, 147
Hessians, 33, 37, 38, 39 sq., 42, 43, 120
Heister, Jos., 84
Heidelberg, Leb. Co., Pa., 120
Henry, Wm., 71, 80, 136, 137
herds, 88
Hodgson, Capt. Alex., 129
Holstein, Matthias, 153
honey-comb stone, 139
hospitals, 34, 35, 63, 75
hunger, 51, 52
Huntingdon, Gen., 57, 59, 71, 136
huts, 24, 25, 54, 55, 56, 57, 58, 66, 88, 92, 93, 95, 96, 124, 137
Howe, Gen., 31, 44, 88, 89, 109
Hughes, John, 89

Indians, 105
Ireland, 77
iron, 28, 29, 30, 31, 87, 88, 92, 97, 99, 100, 101, 103, 120, 140

Jackson, Wm., 120
Jenkins, Mr., 128
" farm, 128
" island, 128
" pool, 128
Jefferson, Thos., 84
Jones, Benj., 87, 96, 119
" Rev. David, 64
" Enoch, 113
" James, 100
" Nathaniel, 113, 114
" Samuel, 58, 81, 82, 113
Jordan, 92

Keugel's Tavern, 82, 113
Kirk, James, 94
Kennedy, Alex., 123, 124, 130
" David R., 130
" John, 130
" Wm., 130
" Port, 130, 131
Kingston, Stephen, 134
Kniphausen, Gen., 33
Knox, Gen., 58, 59, 89, 112
Kosciusko, Gen., 58, 70

Lafayette, Gen., 58, 59, 64, 70, 76, 77, 112, 146, 147
Lancaster, 75
lead, 107, 108, 141
Lee, Col., 37, 38
Lee, Gen., 58, 63, 77, 89, 115
Lewises, 65
lime, 130, 135, 140
loyalists, 42
MacDougal, Gen., 58
Madison, James, 84, 85
Macons, 65
Mann, Jos. (col.), 58
Marlin, Joshua, 102
Marshal, Chief Justice John, 84
Mathachen, 44
Matson's Ford, 60, 89
Maxwell, Gen., 58, 59, 111
McIntosh, Gen., 58, 59, 77
Merchianza, 89
Merion, Upper, 45
Merriwethers, 65
militia, 32
Miller, John, 120
Mifflin, Gen., 39, 58, 59, 64, 77, 97, 119, 121, 150
Miner, Hon. Chas., 59
Montgomery County, 27, 29, 36, 45, 53, 123
Monroe, James, 60
Moore, Anthony, 113
" Elizabeth, 83
" Edwin, 124
" Jane, 83
" Jesse, 53
" John, 57, 80, 87, 123, 124
" John, Jr., 124, 125
" Mordecai, 53, 54, 55, 57, 87, 96, 123, 124
" Richard, 124
" Samuel, 124, 138
Moores, the, 92, 152
Moores Fort, 85
" " Mordecai, 53, 86, 152
" " John, 53, 85
Morgan, Gen., 57, 60, 61, 123
" Mordecai, 60
Morgan's Corner, 61
Morris, Robert, 128, 129
Morrisville, 128
Mount Joy, 27, 38, 121
Mount Misery, 27
Muhlenberg, Gen., 57, 59, 77, 123

Nash, Gen., 44, 59
Nantmeal, 97
New England, 75, 76
New Englanders, 72, 75
Neshaminy Creek, 109
neutrals, 42, 43, 109, 117

New York, 45
Norris Manor, 110
Norristown, 29, 36
North, Caleb, 38, 120, 121
North Carolina, 44
Nutt, Samuel, 27
Nutt's Road, 27, 100

observatory, 104
officers, 56, 58, 71, 74, 79, 80, 81, 82, 95, 107, 114, 118, 123, 129
Owen, Robert, 100

Park, the, 60
pasturage, 143
Patterson, Gen., 82
Paul, Jacob, 100
" Joseph, 100
Paoli, 26, 33, 75, 77
Pawling (Pauling) family, 107
" Henry, 36, 72, 107, 133
" Levi, 72, 107, 133
" Nathan, 36
" Wm., 107, 108
Pauling's Bridge, 107
" Ford, 36
peace, 97, 98, 126, 155
Penn, Wm., 128
" Letitia, 128
" Letitia's Manor, 128
Pennsylvania, 92
pensions, 80, 87, 133
Peacock, Ralph, 101
Peters, Richard, 84
" Judge, 145
Philadelphia, 26, 27, 31, 33, 34, 38, 44, 79, 86, 88, 89, 91, 97, 99, 101, 124, 126
pension, 80
Perkiomen Creek, 44, 108, 109
Phillips, Jonathan, 114
Pickering, Timothy, 84
pickets, 54, 88, 92, 96, 123
picket guard, 112
Pineville, N. J., 81
Poland, 70
Poor, Gen., 58, 59, 115, 119
Porter, Andrew, 133
" Gov. David E., 133
Potter, Gen., 59, 119
Potts, family of, 29, 31
" David, 29, 31, 99, 100, 101, 104
" Isaac, 29, 31, 59-65, 99, 100
" James, 101
" John, 29
Pottsgrove, 29
Pottstown, 29
Pittsgrove, N. J., 80
provost, 57
" guard, 133

provisions, 31, 74, 79, 87, 95
Proctor, Col., 59, 60
Prussia, 68, 69, 70
Pugh, Mary, 81
Pulaski, Gen., 58, 70, 115

rafts, 37
Rambo, (Canoe) John, 34
rangers, 57, 60
Reading, 75, 119
Reading Railroad, 27, 100, 131, 132, 135
Rear Line Hill, 54, 58, 59, 63, 86, 104
rebels, 31, 40
Rebel Hill, 60
Record, The Village, 59
redoubt, 59
Reese, Mrs. Elizabeth, 69, 80
" George, 61
" Griffith, 61
" John, 60
religion, 25, 39, 43, 47, 50, 64, 65, 97, 109, 115, 117, 129
relics, 91
Republican, 36
Ridge Road, 36
Richardson, Eleanor, 137
Richard, Samuel, 33, 58, 81, 82, 111, 113, 114
Riley, David, 129
Roberts, Hon. Jonathan, 148
" Matthew, 110
Robinson, Col. Thomas, 116, 117
Rodgers, Charles, 104
" & Co., 102
" John, 102, 103, 104
Rogers, Rev. Wm., 39
royalists, 30, 31, 36, 37, 42, 43, 44, 46
Russia, 70
Ryan, Major, 116, 117

Savannah, 70
Schuylkill County, 105
" Falls of, 35, 36
" river, 27, 31, 34, 45, 52, 53, 54, 59, 60, 72, 73, 89, 90, 92, 100, 107, 108, 124, 125, 152
Scott, Gen., 82, 113
secret doors, 101
Sernea, Gen., 82
shoes, 49, 62
Shur, Michael, 57, 129, 134
Shannonville (now Audubon), 108
Sharpless, Isaac, 134, 135
" John, 112
Shearer, John, 108
sick, the, 75, 121
Skippack, 33, 44
slavery, 41, 50
small-pox, 62, 75, 117, 118

Smallwood, Gen., 58, 59
Smith, Provost Wm., 57, 128, 138
" Samuel, 94
" Gen. Samuel, 73
Southerners, 63, 65
South, the, 80
springs of water, 125, 129, 130, 132
spy, 31, 37, 79
State Road, 82, 112, 113
Stephens, Dr. Abijah, 42, 51, 57, 67, 70, 87, 95, 96, 121, 122, 143
" Abijah, Jr., 137
" adhesive plaster, 122
" Benj., 40
" Elizabeth, 83
" David, 53, 55, 57, 73, 80, 85, 96, 97, 128, 136, 143
" (Fort), 54, 85
" family, 28, 70, 92, 152
" Grandmother, 50, 51, 52, 81, 83
" Jehu, 35, 38, 107
" Maurice, 71, 136
" Sarah, 36
" Stephen, 39, 122
" Wm., 137
Sterling, Gen. Lord, 60, 69, 115
Steuben, Baron, 58, 70, 71, 137
Steuben's Kitchen, 71
stores, military, 31, 32, 33, 37, 38, 79, 89
Stony Creek, 36
Sullivan, Gen., 58, 59, 64, 72, 73, 77, 119, 120, 150
Sullivan's Bridge, 72, 73, 107, 137
surgery, 96
Sutcliffe, Robert, 110
Susquehanna river, 47
Swede's Ford, 34, 36

tavern, 35
Thomson, Archibald, 36
" Rev. Chas., 155
timber, 30, 41, 54, 74, 87, 95, 96, 101, 102, 143, 145
Tories, 42, 90, 117
Towamencin, 44
Trumbull, Col., 84

University of Pa., 39, 57

Valley Creek, 27, 53, 54, 58, 59, 70, 86, 87, 102, 103, 115
Valley forge, the, 24, 25, 26, 27, 92, 93, 97, 98, 120
Valley Forge estate, 20, 28, 29, 38, 54, 55, 99, 115, 136
Valley, the Great, 32, 57, 58, 75, 87, 92, 111, 113, 125, 152
Valley Road, 27

Vanderslice, Thomas, 108
Varnum, Gen., 57, 59, 84, 137
Vaux, James, 109
Virginia, 50
Vodges, Jacob, 101, 102

Wagstaff, Hugh, 103
Wales, 28
Walker, Enoch, 118
" Mrs. Elizabeth, 82
" Hanniah, 120
" Isaac, 28, 58, 76, 81, 116, 117 118
" Jacob, 87, 119
" Joseph, 87, 96 115, 116, 117, 118
" Lewis, 28, 113, 114, 115, 116, 117, 118
" Richard C., 116, 135
" Sarah, 83
" Thomas, 116, 134
" Wm., 116
Walkers, the, 92, 152
Walters, Jacob, 58
Wanwag, Lewis, 130
War of 1812, 84
Waters, Thomas, 32, 34, 38, 40, 41, 42, 87, 96, 119, 120
Watson, John, 89
Watson's Annals, 89

Wayne, Gen. Anthony, 58, 59, 64, 76, 113, 114, 116-118, 121, 148, 150
Wayne, Hon. Isaac, 148, 150
Washington, Gen., 24, 25, 28, 30, 33, 38, 44, 45, 46, 57, 59, 63, 64, 65, 77, 81, 84, 88, 89, 90, 109, 118, 121, 122, 126, 127, 150, 151
Washington, Lady, 64, 118
Weem's History, 65
Weisel, Frederick, 134
Wetherill's, 107, 108
West Chester, 59, 147
Wheedon, Gen., 49, 50, 58, 59, 66, 67, 81
White Horse, 109
Williams, John, 34
Wilson, David, 112
Wissahickon, 89
Woodford, Gen., 82, 113
Woodman, Edward, 30, 87, 109, 126, 127, 150, 151, 157-164
" Mrs. Edward, 168, 150
" Henry, 7-10, 24, 25
Worthington, John, 112
wounded, the, 75

Yellow Springs, 75
York County, 46, 47, 61

Zook, David, 124, 131

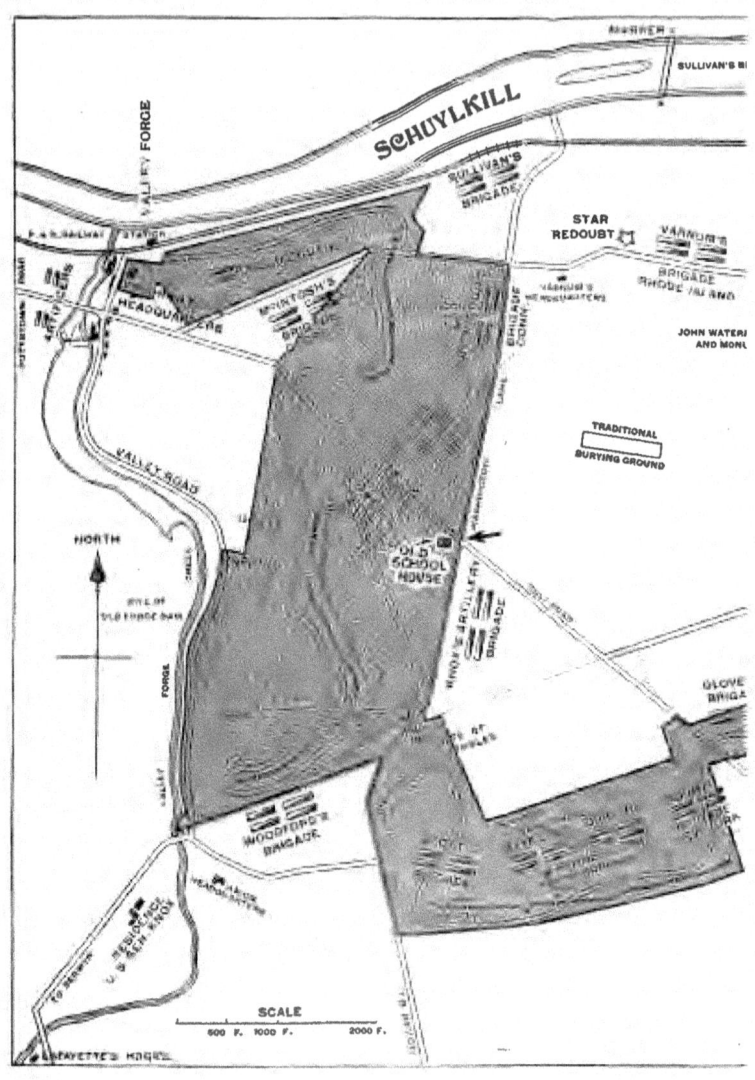

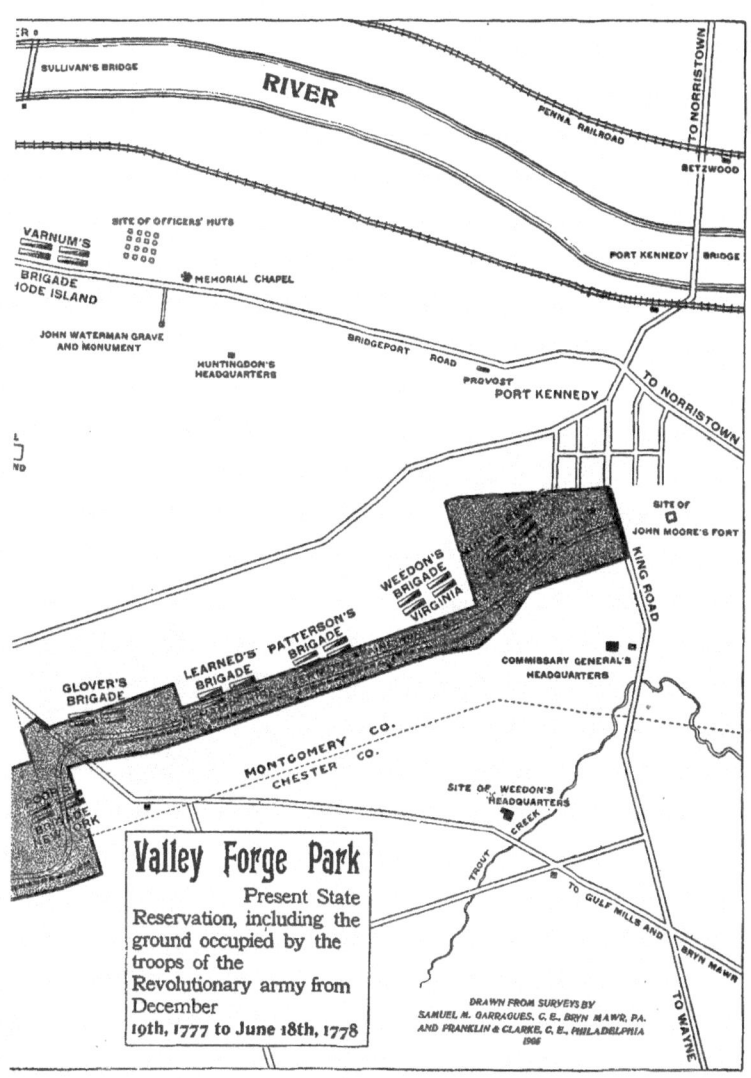

www.ingramcontent.com/pod-product-compliance
Lightning Source LLC
Chambersburg PA
CBHW071447150426
43191CB00008B/1270